A Leeds Playhouse, Curve ... ,urch
co-p.

# by Frances Poet

Associate Production Sponsor at Leeds Playhouse

jmglendinning
Insurance Brokers

*Maggie May* was first performed at Queen's Theatre Hornchurch
on 13 March 2020.

All performances of *Maggie May* are dementia-friendly.

## Cast

| | |
|---|---|
| MAGGIE | **Eithne Browne** |
| GORDON | **John McArdle** |
| JO | **Maxine Finch** |
| MICHAEL | **Mark Holgate** |
| CLAIRE | **Shireen Farkhoy** |

## Creatives

| | |
|---|---|
| Writer | **Frances Poet** |
| Director | **Jemima Levick** |
| Set & Costume Designer | **Francis O'Connor** |
| Assistant Designer | **Alex Green** |
| Lighting Designer | **Chris Davey** |
| Composer & Sound Designer | **Claire McKenzie** |
| Assistant Director | **Anna Marshall** |
| Casting Director | **Kay Magson** CDG |
| Theatre & Dementia Advisor | **Nicky Taylor** |
| Movement Coach | **Dr Joseph Mercier** |
| Dialect Coach | **Jamie Matthewman** |
| | |
| Company Stage Manager | **Julie Issott** |
| Deputy Stage Manager | **Robyn Hardisty** |
| Assistant Stage Manager | **Sandrine Enryd Carlsson** |

Show created by Leeds Playhouse & Queen's Theatre Hornchurch Production teams with support from Curve

Thank you to our consultants living with dementia and their supporters who have guided us through the process of making *Maggie May*:

**Bob Fulcher**, **Pete Grogan** & **Jan Ellis**, **Mick** & **Lyn Haith**, **Eugene Harris** & **Diana Smith-Harris**, **Peter** & **Nancy Jervis**, **Wendy Mitchell**, **Rosa Peterson**, **Debbie Catley** and **Debbie Marshall**.

# Cast

### Eithne Browne | MAGGIE

Eithne's first appearance was on stage at the Liverpool Playhouse in Willy Russell's *Blood Brothers*. On its transfer to the West End Eithne took over from Barbara Dickson in the lead role for over 50 performances. Not bad for a first job!

Her other favourite stage plays include: *Shirley Valentine* (Northcott Theatre); *Educating Rita* (national tour); *To Kill a Mockingbird* (New Vic Theatre, Stoke); *Stags and Hens* (New Vic, London); *8 Miles High, Alfie, A Pocket Dream* (Octagon Theatre, Bolton); *Billy Liar, A Month in the Country* (Salisbury Playhouse); *Talking Heads* (Arts Academy, Liverpool); *A Sense of Justice* (Perth Repertory Theatre); *The Secret Garden* (Byre Theatre, St Andrews); *Intent to Murder, Say Who You Are, Boeing Boeing* (English Theatre, Vienna); *Limestone Cowboy* (Belgrade Theatre, Coventry); *The Odd Couple, An Awfully Big Aventure, Tartuffe, The Star* (Liverpool Playhouse); *Wuthering Heights* (national tour); *The Full Monty* (national tour); *Vagina Monologues* (Neptune Theatre/Royal Court Liverpool); *GYD Diet, The Sum, Northern Flight* (Everyman Theatre); *Mam I'm 'Ere* (Dome Liverpool); *Tuppence to Cross the Mersey* (Epstein Theatre/tour); *I Am Janet* (Gap Theatre Manchester); *Brick Up the Mersey Tunnels, Lost Soul, Good Golly Miss Molly, Two, Cinderella, Eight Miles High, Night Collar, Dirty Dusting, Merry Ding Dong, Funny Money, Ladies' Day, Masquerade, Special Measures* and *Golden Oldies* (*and teas and coffees*) (Royal Court Liverpool).

TV credits include: Chrissy Rogers in Channel 4's *Brookside*. She has also appeared in: *Mobile, Lillies, Cold Feet* (Granada); *The Royal, Emmerdale* (YTV); *Doctors, Stretford Wives, Clocking Off, Peace Keepers, Having it Off*, the BAFTA award-winning *Room At The Top* (BBC TV) and *Secret State* (BBC).

Eithne was voted Woman of the Year at the 2013/14 Daily Post & Echo Arts & Culture Awards. She is also the voice of the world famous Mersey Ferry.

### John McArdle | GORDON

John McArdle was born in Liverpool a long time ago. He travelled the world as a young man, then decided to settle down and become an actor at the age of twenty-five. He trained at E15 drama school. This is John's first time appearing at Leeds Playhouse and he is looking forward to it.

John has worked in theatre, TV and radio for the past thirty-five years. Some of his favourite theatre credits include: *Lennon* (Liverpool Everyman); *Our Country's Good* (Liverpool Playhouse); *Brassed Off* (York Theatre Royal/national tour); *The Crucible* (Crucible Theatre Sheffield); *The Arbour* (National Theatre); *Two, Oh! What a Lovely War* (Octagon Theatre, Bolton); *Flying Blind* (Library Theatre Manchester); *The Rise and Fall of Little Voice* (tour).

TV credits include: *Brookside*, the Ruth Rendell series *Gallowglass, Waking the Dead, Law & Order UK, Foyle's War, U Be Dead, Waterloo Road, The Cazalets, Blue Murder, The Bill, Prime Suspect 5, Finney, Wycliffe, City Central, Peak Practice, Vera, Merseybeat, Casualty, Holby City, The Beat Goes On, Emmerdale*.

Film credits include: *There's Only One Jimmy Grimble, The Place of the Dead, Revengers Tragedy, Charlie Noades, Rich Deceiver, Thacker, Through My Eyes, The Rochdale Pioneers*.

Radio credits include: *A Clockwork Orange*, amongst many others.

John's autobiography *You Never Said Goodbye* is out now.

**Maxine Finch** | JO

Maxine Finch trained at Dartington College of Arts.

Theatre credits include: *LIT* (HighTide); *State Red* (Hampstead Theatre); Tituba in *The Crucible* (Welsh National Theatre); *Precious* (Theatre Centre); *Unsent Letters* & *In Balance* (Hearth Theatre); *Skybus* (Derby Live); *Getting it Straight* (The Works); *Inside Out of Mind* (Meeting Ground); *All Different, All Equal* (Women in Theatre).

TV credits include: *Trying, Coronation Street, Hollyoaks, Vera, Moving On, DCI Banks, Emmerdale, Eternal Law, Waterloo Road, Blue Murder, The Good Samaritan, Strictly Confidential, New Street Law, Doctors, Guardian, Holby City, Spine Chillers, Burn It, Crossroads* and *Dangerfield*.

Film credits include: *Provoked, A Change in the Weather, The Silver Mask, Martyrs Lane*.

**Mark Holgate** | MICHAEL

Theatre credits include: *Twelfth Night, Hamlet, Macbeth,* A *Midsummer Night's Dream* (Shakespeare's Rose Theatre); *Julius Caesar* (Sheffield Crucible); *The Iliad* (Royal Lyceum Theatre); *The White Devil, The Roaring Girl, All's Well That Ends Well, As You Like It, Hamlet, A Soldier in Every Son, King John, Richard III, Romeo and Juliet (*Royal Shakespeare Company); *The Railway Children* (Waterloo Station); *Observe the Sons of Ulster Marching Toward the Somme* (Hampstead Theatre)*; Troilus & Cressida, Cymbeline* (Cheek by Jowl) and *Women of Troy* (National Theatre).

Television and film credits include: *Emmerdale, Bodyguard, Tina and Bobby, Against the Law, Dark Angel, Cuffs, Lawful Killing, Hollyoaks, Doctors, Coronation Street* and *Atonement*.

Radio credits include: *Drink* and *Fragments*.

**Shireen Farkhoy** | CLAIRE

Shireen Farkhoy trained at Bristol Old Vic Theatre School (2013–15).

Theatre credits include: *Where We Began* (SBC); *The Shed Crew* (Red Ladder/Leeds Playhouse); *Bitched* (Kali Theatre); *Combustion* (Tara Arts); *Haste Ye Back* (Arcola Theatre); *The Collector* (Kathryn Barker Productions); *Sam Wanamaker Festival* (Shakespeare's Globe Theatre); *You:The Player* (West Yorkshire Playhouse); *Hansel and Gretel* (Wakefield Theatre Royal); *Trinity's Church* (West Yorkshire Playhouse); *My Place* (Tutti Frutti) and *Kaahini* (Red Ladder).

TV credits: *Doctors, Vera, The 'A' Word, Waterloo Road* and *The Royal Today*.

# Creative Team

**Frances Poet** | Writer

Frances Poet is a Glasgow-based writer. Stage plays include *Fibres* (Stella Quines/Citizens Theatre, Scottish tour 2019); *Gut* (Writers' Guild Best Play Award winner, UK Theatre Best Play Award nominated and Bruntwood Prize for Playwriting shortlisted, Traverse Theatre and Tron Theatre 2018 and in a French translation as *Madra*, Théâtre La Licorne, Montréal 2019 and Théâtre Périscope, Quebec 2020) and the multi-award-winning *Adam* (Scottish and UK tours 2017/18, NYU Skirball Centre 2019 and Gasworks Arts Park, Melbourne 2020).

Frances has also completed a number of classic adaptations including *The Macbeths* (Citizens Theatre/Scottish tour 2017/18); *What Put The Blood* (Abbey Theatre, Dublin 2017 and previously as *Andromaque*, Scottish tour 2015); *Dance of Death* (Citizens Theatre 2016) and *The Misanthrope* (Óran Mòr 2014).

Radio work includes *Alt Delete* (BBC Radio 3, 2019); *Gut* (BBC Radio 4, 2019) and *The Disappointed* (BBC Radio Scotland 2015). Screen work includes episodes of *River City* and several short films that have played at national and international festivals.

Frances's play *Crusaders* is part of NT Connections 2020 and her adaptation of Jane Austen's *Sense and Sensibility* opens at Pitlochry Festival Theatre in August 2020.

**Jemima Levick** | Director

Jemima Levick trained at Queen Margaret University, Edinburgh and on a Scottish Arts Council Director Traineeship at the Royal Lyceum Theatre, Edinburgh.

She is Artistic Director & Chief Executive of Stellar Quines, a touring theatre company based in Scotland. She has won and been nominated for a number of awards and has directed more than 35 professional productions.

Her credits for Stellar Quines include: *Fibres* (with the Citizens Theatre); *This Girl Laughs, This Girl Cries, This Girl Does Nothing* (with Imaginate) *Bingo!* (with Grid Iron); *The Lover* (with the Royal Lyceum and Scottish Dance Theatre); *The 306: Day* (with Perth Theatre and The National Theatre of Scotland).

Prior to Stellar Quines, she was Artistic Director at Dundee Rep where she directed more than 20 productions. Highlights include: *All My Sons, Great Expectations, The Glass Menagerie, Time and the Conways, The Tempest, A Doll's House, Equus, The Elephant Man* and *Beauty and the Beast.*

As director and producer she has worked with a number of other companies, including BBC Studios, The Royal Lyceum, The National Theatre of Scotland, Borderline, The Traverse Theatre and Paines Plough.

Future projects include: *River City, Molly & Mack* (both BBC) and a UK wide tour of *Fibres*.

**Francis O'Connor** | Set & Costume Designer

Francis O'Connor trained at Wimbledon School of Art.

Recent theatre includes: *Richard III* (Lincoln Centre, New York); *What's in a Name* (Birmingham/tour); *The Beacon* (Druid, Galway and Dublin); *Epiphany* (Druid, Galway); *The Country Girls* (Abbey, Dublin); *The Tell-Tale Heart* (National Theatre); Patrick Barlow's *Messiah* (Birmingham/The Other Palace, London); *Richard III* (Druid, Galway, & Dublin); *Waiting for Godot* (Edinburgh Festival/US tour); *Sive* (Galway); *The Arabian Nights* (Lyceum, Edinburgh); *King of the Castle* (Druid, Galway & Dublin); *Private Lives* (Gate, Dublin); *Beauty Queen of Leenane* (Ireland, Los Angeles, New York).

Recent musical and opera includes: *Bluebeard* (Biel, Switzerland); *Parade* (Théâtre du Châtelet, Paris); *Gypsy* (Royal Exchange Theatre, Manchester); *Fantasio* (Garsington Opera); *Angela's Ashes* (Dublin/tour); *Die Entfuhrung aus dem Serail* (Monte Carlo); *Kiss Me Kate* (Bonn Opera); various productions for Grange Park Opera including *Porgy and Bess*, *Oklahoma*, *Roméo and Juliette* and *Tosca*; *Figaro* (Irish National Opera/ Wexford/Dublin); *Iolanthe* (Biel, Switzerland); *The Magic Flute* (Ekaterinburg, Russia); *Il Turco in Italia* (Garsington Opera); *Farnace*, *Waiting for Godot* (Spoleto Festival, Charleston); *Don Giovanni* (Nederlandse Reisopera); *The Wedding Singer* (Leicester/ national tour).

Work in hand includes: *The Cherry Orchard* (Druid, Galway & Dublin); *Street Scene* (Opera North); *La Gioconda* and *Meet Me In St Louis* (Grange Park Opera).

Awards include: three Irish Times Awards, Boston Globe and Critics' Circle Awards. His designs for the opera *Pinocchio* nominated for Germany's Der Faust Prize.

**Chris Davey** | Lighting Designer

For West Yorkshire Playhouse: *Villette*, *Sweeney Todd*, *The Wind in the Willows*, *Waiting for Godot*, *King Lear*, *The Deep Blue Sea*, *Death of a Salesman*, *The Count of Monte Cristo*, *The Caucasian Chalk Circle*, *Dial M for Murder*, *Blues in the Night*, *Twelfth Night*, *The Wizard of Oz*, *Dangerous Corner*, *Johnson Over Jordon*, *Broken Glass*, *The Comedy of Errors* and *Half a Sixpence*.

He has designed extensively for the National Theatre, Royal Shakespeare Company, Shared Experience Theatre, Royal Court, Hampstead Theatre, Lyric Hammersmith, Royal Exchange Theatre, Manchester, West Yorkshire Playhouse, Royal Lyceum Edinburgh, Citizens's Theatre Glasgow, Birmingham Rep and Manchester International Festival.

Designs include: *Touching the Void* (tour/Duke of York's Theatre, London); *Witness for the Prosecution* (County Hall, London); *Switzerland* (Bath Theatre Royal/Ambassadors Theatre, London); *Nightfall* (Bridge Theatre, London); *Rhinoceros* (Edinburgh International Festival); *Vamos Cuba!* (Sadler's Wells); *Sweeney Todd* (La Monnaie, Brussels); *42nd Street* (Chicago Lyric Opera/ Théâtre du Châtelet, Paris); Matthew Bourne's *The Car Man* and *Lord of the Flies* (Sadler's Wells/national and international tours); *The Driver's Seat* (National Theatre of Scotland); *Carlos Acosta's Classical Selection* (Coliseum/ Royal Albert Hall/world tour); *The Crucible*, *Wonderful Town*, *The History Boys*, *High Society*, *Dr Dolittle* and *Dial M for Murder* (national tours); *Secret Seven*, *A Little Night Music*, *The Crucible*, *The Suicide*, *Blue Stockings*, *Miss Julie* (Storyhouse, Chester).

**Claire McKenzie** | Composer & Sound Designer

Claire McKenzie trained at the Royal Conservatoire of Scotland where she received the Patrons Prize for Composition and the Paul Kelly Prize for Drama. She now works as a Composer and Musical Director in the UK and internationally.

Claire is one half of musical writing team, Noisemaker, along with writer Scott Gilmour. Most recently their musical, *Hi, My Name is Ben* premiered at Goodspeed Musicals, Connecticut and the NAMT Festival in NYC. The pair were named as one of the New Voices by Walt Disney Imagineering and have written several musicals produced in the UK and the US.

Other credits include: *Oor Wullie, The Snow Queen, Little Red and the Wolf* (Dundee Rep); *My Left/Right Foot, 306:Day* (National Theatre of Scotland); *Legend Trippers* (National Youth Music Theatre); *Songs for the Seven Hills, What We Wished For* (Sheffield Crucible); *The Caucasian Chalk Circle, The Iliad, The Lion, the Witch and the Wardrobe, The BFG* (Edinburgh Lyceum); *Long Day's Journey into Night, Hansel and Gretel, Beauty and the Beast* (Citizens Theatre); *Atlantic: A Scottish Story* (winner, Herald Angel Award 2017); *Forest Boy* (New York Musical Festival); *The Girl Who* (Merry-Go-Round Playhouse, NYC). www.noisemaker.org.uk

**Anna Marshall** | Assistant Director

Anna Marshall is a Lecoq trained director currently undertaking the MFA in Theatre Directing at Birkbeck University.

Her recent directing credits include: *Mustard Doesn't Go With Girls* (Lyric Hammersmith Studio, Pleasance); *Filth* by Irvine Welsh (Tristan Bates); *Havisham* (Theatre503); *Rounds* (Bolton Octagon) and *Just Lose It* (Jersey Opera House). She has also toured work to China, France and the North of England. She is particularly interested in championing new voices and is a founder of Bric a Brac Theatre Company.

**Kay Magson** CDG | Casting Director

Theatre credits include: *The Solid Gold Cadillac* (Garrick Theatre); *Dangerous Corner* (West Yorkshire Playhouse/West End); *Round the Horne… Revisited, Dracula* (national tours); *Singin' in the Rain* (West Yorkshire Playhouse/NT/ national tour); *Aspects of Love, All the Fun of the Fair* and *The Witches of Eastwick* (national tours); *Breakfast at Tiffany's* (national tour/WE); *Kes* (Liverpool/national tour); *Martin Guerre* (WYP/ national tour); *Great Expectations* (ETT/Watford/national tour); *James and the Giant Peach, Gangsta Granny* and *Horrible Histories* (Birmingham Stage Company); *Sweeney Todd* (Royal Festival Hall).

Kay was resident at the West Yorkshire Playhouse for seventeen years where she cast many shows including *Hamlet*, The McKellen Ensemble Season, the Patrick Stewart Priestley Season and many others, She casts regularly for Curve where she is an Associate Artist and for Derby Theatre, Storyhouse, Liverpool Everyman, Birmingham Stage Company and many others.

Kay is a member of the Casting Director's Guild of Great Britain (CDG).

**Nicky Taylor** | Theatre and Dementia Advisor

Nicky is Theatre and Dementia Research Associate at Leeds Playhouse, leading ground-breaking creative practice with people living with dementia. She initiated and directed Every Third Minute (2018), a pioneering theatre festival curated by people living with dementia, and facilitated the co-authorship of three plays by people with dementia and professional writing partners. The festival's creative co-production process forms the basis of her doctoral research at Leeds Beckett University's Centre for Dementia Research.

She created the world's first Dementia Friendly Performance in 2014 and has authored a best-practice guide to staging dementia-friendly productions. She supports the theatre industry, nationally and internationally, to involve and value people with dementia as creative equals. Her work has been recognised with major national awards from Arts & Business, The Alzheimer's Society and National Dementia Care Awards.

Nicky was the Playhouse's Community Development Manager for 12 years, during which she conceived and produced the UK's first Relaxed Performance for learning disabled audiences (2009).

She is a Churchill Fellow, travelling internationally to share practice in arts and dementia, and a member of UK Dementia Congress advisory group. Nicky's work as a carer, supporting people in their own homes and in care homes, was integral to forming her ethos of working with and learning from people living with dementia.

**Dr Joseph Mercier** | Movement Coach

Education: Lecturer in Creative & Contextual Studies, PhD in Dance, Performance and Queer Studies (Practice Based), Royal Central School of Speech and Drama, MA Advanced Theatre Practice (Directing), Royal Central School of Speech and Drama, BFA Theatre with a Concentration in Playwriting.

Joseph Mercier's dance practice is rooted in a love of thinking through the body. His study of choreographic and dramaturgy processes is animated by his interests in performance politics and queer subcultures. His teaching and research practice is playfully rigorous and rigorously playful.

Professional activity and research interests: 2018, Speaker at Performing Gender Week, Yorkshire Dance, 2018, Questioning the Contemporary Research Salon with Beth Cassani, Martin Hargreaves and Frauke Requardt, Leeds Beckett University. 2018, Convenor, Leeds Beckett University, Performance Research Happy Hour, Leeds Beckett University/Live Art Bistro. 2017, Research Residency and Seminar with Prof. Emilyn Claid, Leeds Beckett University. 2016, Prologue Research Residency with Mark Ravenhill, Arts Admin.

Performance artefacts: 2018, *Faun* (working title), work-in-progress collaboration with Beth Cassani. 2017, *Fox and the Hound*, PanicLab, co-director and performer, in association with Live Art Bistro. 2016, *Theseus Beefcake*, PanicLab with Jordan Tannahill, commissioned by The Albany, Homotopia. 2016, *Swan Lake II: Dark Waters*, PanicLab. 2015, *R.I.O.T.*, PanicLab, commissioned by Dance City, in association with Cambridge Junction, MDI, Unity Theatre. 2013 *Rite of Spring*, PanicLab, commissioned by Birthday Rites at Chisenhale Dance Space.

**Jamie Matthewman** | Dialect Coach

Jamie Matthewman is a voice, dialect and acting coach working in film, TV, theatre, education and the corporate world.

He trained as an actor, and subsequently as a voice and dialect coach, at the Guildhall School of Music and Drama.

He loves teaching dialect through physicality, rhythm, tune, energy and the world of the accent, as well as through more specific linguistic features.

He is also currently training to be a Feldenkrais practitioner. This neuromuscular education method is wonderful for increasing awareness of breath, speech muscles and resonant placement and improving deeper listening.

Some of the actors that Jamie has worked include Gary Oldman, Kristen Scott Thomas, Ben Mendelsohn, Lily James, Ralph Fiennes, Carey Mulligan and Vanessa Hudgens. He has coached at the Royal Shakespeare Company, the Royal Court, Leeds Playhouse, Opera North and taught in several London drama schools including Guildhall, Drama Centre, Arts Ed, ALRA and, also, Florida State University.

## CO-PRODUCED BY

There has been a Playhouse in Leeds for almost 50 years; from 1970 to 1990 as Leeds Playhouse, then, with the opening of a new theatre on its current Quarry Hill site it became West Yorkshire Playhouse until reclaiming its original name in 2018.

Leeds Playhouse is one of the UK's leading producing theatres; a cultural hub, a place where people gather to tell and share stories and to engage in world class theatre. It makes work which is pioneering and relevant, seeking out the best companies and artists to create inspirational theatre in the heart of Yorkshire. From large-scale spectacle to intimate performance we develop and make work for our stages, for found spaces, for touring, for schools and community centres. We create work to entertain and inspire.

As dedicated collaborators, we work regularly with other organisations from across the UK, independent producers, and some of the most distinctive, original voices in theatre today. Through our Furnace programme, we develop work with established practitioners and find, nurture and support new voices that ought to be heard. We cultivate artists by providing creative space for writers, directors, companies and individual theatre makers to refine their practice at any stage of their career.

Alongside our work for the stage we are dedicated to providing creative engagement opportunities that excite and stimulate. We build, run and sustain projects which reach out to everyone from refugee communities, to young people and students, to older communities and people with learning disabilities. At the Playhouse there is always a way to get involved.

### Leeds Playhouse – Vital Theatre

Artistic Director **James Brining**
Executive Director **Robin Hawkes**
Chairman of the Board **Sir Rodney Brooke CBE**
Find us on Facebook: **Leeds Playhouse**
Follow us on Twitter: **@LeedsPlayhouse**
Follow us on Instagram: **@LeedsPlayhouse**

**LeedsPlayhouse.org.uk**

Leeds Theatre Trust Limited Charity Number 255460
VAT No. 545 4890 17 Company No. 926862, England Wales
Registered address Playhouse Square, Quarry Hill, Leeds, LS2 7UP

### Major Funders

**Principal Capital and Families Partner**     **Principal Capital and Access Partner**

CaddickGroup.                                    ⟨IM⟩ irwinmitchell

**We are grateful to all supporters of Leeds Playhouse, whose dedication makes our vital work possible, both on and off stage.**

# QUEEN'S THEATRE
### HORNCHURCH

Queen's Theatre Hornchurch (QTH) is a vibrant producing theatre, working in Outer East London, Essex and beyond. As a cultural hub, over 210,000 people enjoy the programme each year. Audiences are guaranteed a warm welcome from a three year winner of UK Theatre's Most Welcoming Theatre (2016 – 2018) and London Theatre of the Year 2020 (The Stage Awards), the first Outer London theatre to receive this prestigious award.

Since the appointment of Douglas Rintoul as Artistic Director and Mathew Russell as Executive Director, productions have included the record-breaking regional premiere of *Priscilla, Queen of the Desert*, and critically acclaimed regional premieres of musicals *Made in Dagenham* and *Once*, both co-produced with the New Wolsey Ipswich, with *Once* now on a 6-month national tour. QTH world premiered a commissioned adaptation of *The Invisible Man* by Clem Garritty and *Abi* by Atiha Sen Gupta, co-produced with Derby Theatre.

Productions are seen on tour by more than 40,000 people each year. *The Crucible*, co-produced with Selladoor Productions, undertook a 5-month tour, a major revival of *Kindertransport* was produced in an innovative international partnership with Les Théâtres de la Ville de Luxembourg, *Abigail's Party* was co-produced with Derby Theatre and Salisbury Playhouse, and the musical *The Hired Man* with Hull Truck Theatre and Oldham Coliseum.

QTH is at the heart of the local community, and offers a wide range of life-enhancing workshops and classes for people of all ages – working with more than 34,000 participants last year. QTH was Theatre partner to the National Theatre for Public Acts, a new landmark initiative to create extraordinary acts of theatre and community, producing the European premiere of the musical adaptation of *As You Like It*, which saw 149 participants from across London's diverse communities experiencing a life-changing performance on QTH's stage.

QTH talent development programme, Outer Limits, connects with local and regional professional artists, offering essential support that hasn't previously existed. Essex on Stage is an ambitious programme led by QTH, championing positive notions of Essex, and celebrating theatre made by working-class people, made possible by the Theatre receiving the 2018 Clothworkers' Foundation Theatre Award. This was launched with the regional premiere of David Eldridge's *In Basildon* and an ambitious rep season, offering the world premiere of Sadie Hasler's *Stiletto Beach* and London premiere of Luke Norris' *So Here We Are*.

Situated in the borough with the 4th lowest arts engagement in London, QTH has led a successful consortium bid for £1 million of new Creative People and Places funding, towards Havering Changing, a partnership seeking radical new ideas to engage local communities in arts and culture. Last year, an astonishing 45% of QTH's audience were new to the Theatre.

**queens-theatre.co.uk** Twitter: **@queenstheatreh** Instagram: **@queenstheatrehornchurch**
Facebook **@QueensTheatreH**

Havering Theatre Trust Ltd established in 1953.
Queen's Theatre Hornchurch, Billet Lane, Hornchurch, RM11 1QT
Registered in England No 524845. Registered Charity No 248680 VAT No 246 7715 38

Welcome.

Opened by Her Majesty The Queen, Curve is a spectacular state-of-the-art theatre based in the heart of Leicester's vibrant Cultural Quarter.

Over recent years, we have developed a reputation for producing, programming and touring a bold and diverse programme of musicals, plays, new work, dance and opera. All of this is presented alongside a dynamic mix of community engagement, a vibrant youth theatre, artist development and learning programmes, which firmly places audiences, artists and communities at the heart of everything we do.

In 2019, three Curve-originated productions played London's West End – *On Your Feet!* (London Coliseum), Sue Townsend's *The Secret Diary of Adrian Mole Aged 13¾ – The Musical* (The Ambassadors Theatre) and Irving Berlin's *White Christmas* (Dominion Theatre).

As well as a variety of visiting productions, we produce work under our Made at Curve banner, which is recognised by audiences as high quality, provocative and entertaining theatre. Recent Made at Curve productions include Frantic Assembly and Theatre Royal Plymouth's *I Think We Are Alone*; a major, critically acclaimed revival of *West Side Story*; a world premiere adaption of Giles Andreae and Guy Parker Rees' *Giraffes Can't Dance* (co-produced with Rose Theatre Kingston & UK tour); the world premiere of Hanif Kureishi's *My Beautiful Laundrette* (co-produced with Belgrade Theatre Coventry, Everyman Theatre Cheltenham and Leeds Playhouse); a critically acclaimed reprisal of John Osborne's seminal work *The Entertainer* (co-produced with Anthology Theatre & Simon Friend & UK tour); a new UK tour of Jim Jacobs & Warren Casey's *Grease* (2019, 2020 & 2021 UK tours); The 'Best Regional Production' (WhatsOnStage Awards 2020) of Alice Walker's *The Color Purple* (co-produced with Birmingham Hippodrome); Gloria and Emilio Estefan's *On Your Feet!*; Irving Berlin's *White Christmas*; Dr. Seuss's *The Cat in the Hat* (& UK tour) and the multi-award-winning world premiere of Dougal Irvine's adaption of Riaz Khan's *Memoirs of an Asian Football Casual*.

Curve is a registered charity, and this supports our work with people of all ages and backgrounds, enabling them to access, participate in and learn from the arts, nurturing new and emerging talent and creating outstanding, award-winning experiences. Ensuring our theatre is fully accessible, egalitarian and celebrating people from all backgrounds is paramount to our work and the ethos which underpins the entire organisation.

The relationship between artists and audiences is brought together by the extraordinary architecture of our unique home.

**Welcome to our theatre, a theatre for all.**

**Chris Stafford**       **Nikolai Foster**
Chief Executive      Artistic Director

Curve 60 Rutland St, Leicester LE1 1SB **www.curveonline.co.uk**

Twitter: **@CurveLeicester** Facebook: **/CURVEtheatreLeicester** Instagram: **@Curve_Leicester**

Curve is run by Leicester Theatre Trust Limited, a registered charity (no. 230708). We gratefully acknowledge and welcome the continued support of and partnership with the below organisations:

# Acknowledgements

Thank you to all the people living with dementia and their supporters who enliven and enrich our theatre community with their creativity, laughter and determination, and whose stories are the roots of *Maggie May*. There are too many individuals to mention by name and some people who are no longer able to give permission for their names to be included. We have learned from every conversation, opinion, gesture and laugh.

Thanks in particular to the following groups which have offered support, time and energy to the development of *Maggie May*: Leeds City Council's Peer Support Service for people living with dementia, Leeds Playhouse's Our Time group and the Peer Support Cultural Partnership group, Every Third Minute festival curators and our dedicated volunteers.

Thank you to everyone who has contributed stories to The Listening Booth, an interactive front of house installation amplifying the voices of people living with dementia, that accompanies the production in Hornchurch, Leeds and Leicester.

And thank you to everyone who has joined us for a dementia-friendly performance, building the case for audience members with dementia to have continued access to theatre.

*Maggie May* was originally commissioned as part of Every Third Minute – a festival of theatre, dementia and hope – which was funded through a Celebrating Age grant from Arts Council England and The Baring Foundation.

**The Baring Foundation**

# How *Maggie May* came to life – reflections on the process

*By Nicky Taylor, Rosa Peterson and Frances Poet*

## NICKY

Sharing stories is a powerful way to understand dementia, one of the major global health challenges of our times. In telling those stories, we risk presenting an unbalanced perspective by excluding the very people living with the condition.

Traditional stage, screen and media representations of dementia tend to portray a tragic narrative of loss and decline: presenting people with dementia as a burden, and stripping people of their agency at the point of diagnosis. There is no doubt that dementia brings tremendous challenges and losses as it progresses. Yet we must allow space for hope, particularly in the crucial early stages of adapting to a diagnosis, when people want to use their skills and feel purposeful. By failing to acknowledge the things that people with dementia *can* and *do* contribute, these tragic representations of dementia fuel ongoing stigma and stereotypes.

I established the Theatre and Dementia programme at Leeds Playhouse in 2010 to engage people with dementia creatively and collaboratively, harnessing their resilience and determination to forge a creative connection with the world. I have been constantly inspired by people living with dementia and their supporters who negotiate life with dementia, adapting to new challenges every day.

I've found that welcoming people with dementia as creative equals and involving them as decision-makers, advisors, curators and artists, helps them to thrive. It has also transformed the Playhouse's collaborative approach and the stories we tell. Engaging deeply with individual lived experiences of dementia has enabled the co-creation of new models of practice including dementia-friendly performances and Every Third Minute – a festival of theatre, dementia and hope curated by people with dementia.

*Maggie May* was commissioned as part of Every Third Minute to highlight just how much people with dementia, like Maggie, have to offer. They remain a part of the daily lives of their families, fulfilling roles as partner, parent, friend and confidante. Inspiration came from the people attending dementia-friendly activities at Leeds Playhouse who demonstrate this with warmth, humour and solidarity. This story of ordinary people dealing with extraordinary challenges is rooted in Leeds, in the power of music and the strength gained through acceptance and hope.

Frances Poet's incredible talent, empathy and dedication made her the perfect writer to realise this important project. She committed to engaging with people taking part in the Playhouse's activities, listening sensitively and carefully to find the essence of Maggie in the real-life stories of people living with dementia and those supporting them. She has woven the spirit of these stories into the fabric of her beautiful script.

Rosa Peterson is one of the talented people who took on a new adventure as an Every Third Minute festival curator after a diagnosis of vascular dementia. She carries on, despite dementia, with a no-nonsense attitude, using coping strategies she's developed, and supporting others. She's a real-life Maggie May, at the heart of a busy life of family and friendships, a source of strength to everyone around her.

## ROSA

Having dementia is like a rollercoaster. There are up days and there are down days. And it's like that every day. It's life. You're coping with it every day. And you just have to carry on.

Every experience of dementia is different. Some of us can do a lot and some of us can't do as much. Lots of people think you can't do anything if you have dementia. I try and do as much as I can. People ask me why I'm always going out, and I say, 'I'm going to my group because I need to go.' I have to keep going, keep seeing people, otherwise I'd stop, and I wouldn't start again. It's that important. You've got to have hope.

Join a group. It will be hard the first time you go but you'll meet other people who are going through what you're going through. And you'll laugh. You might cry a bit too, but mostly you'll laugh. We laugh a lot. If I feel down, I come to a group, or I talk to a friend. I've always supported other people, and that hasn't changed because I've got dementia. And I like supporting people, but sometimes people think you can do everything you used to do, so that can be hard.

Being involved with *Maggie May* has been brilliant. I've loved it. It's about everyday life and we're living it. I hope when people see it, it makes them more understanding and more patient.

I've found some coping strategies. Keep going, keep doing things, get out, see people who understand, look at the trees, look up at the sky and the stars. Find your way to keep going.

## FRANCES

When I was first invited to talk to Nicky and the team at Leeds Playhouse about writing a play that told a positive story of life after diagnosis, for people living with dementia and their supporters, I was more than a little intimidated by the brief. My dear dad had dementia and there was not much that was positive about our experience as a family, supporting him through it. I didn't know then to seek out groups where he could meet other people with the condition. I didn't know it was possible to find creative, nurturing spaces where he could make significant contributions. So it was with trepidation that I accepted the commission to write *Maggie May*.

I need not have worried. From the moment Nicky introduced me to the extraordinary people living with dementia who were connecting with the Playhouse in various ways – funny, open, interesting and resilient people –

I knew I could write the play. And so Maggie was born, a feisty, funny, no-nonsense Leeds woman who carried the spirit of all these people who had inspired me and been so generous in the way they shared their stories.

But *Maggie May* wasn't written simply by meeting a group of people and incorporating their stories. Nicky set up a highly collaborative development process in which people living with dementia, and their supporters, had a significant dramaturgical input at every stage. Early meetings involved discussions about how colour could be a useful way to identify a character (hence Claire's gold trainers), how narrative reminders could guide an audience member who might otherwise struggle to follow its thread and how music might support this, giving joyful breathing space to an audience having to work hard to hold on to the story. The first reading highlighted that ending the first half on a moment of jeopardy wasn't going to be useful in this piece where the interval is a valid moment for audiences to leave, having still enjoyed their outing. Other incisive feedback has shaped the perspective and tone of the play. *Maggie May* has been a genuinely collaborative process from first to last, shaped by people with dementia for people with dementia.

And it's for this reason, because of the care with which this play has been crafted for its specific audience, that I am particularly excited to watch the play in production. In the first reading, I was sitting behind a man living with dementia who was vocal in his enjoyment of the jokes and songs. It was suggested at the beginning that he might not manage to stay for the second half – but he did, and at the moment in which Maggie explains to her son that though she might not always remember his face or name, her heart will always know him, this audience member turned to look at his wife and gave her a nod to say, 'That's how I feel about you.' It was a special moment. And the reason the play was written.

# MAGGIE MAY

Frances Poet

## Acknowledgements

This play wouldn't exist without Nicky Taylor, who instigated the project and supported it at every stage with the same sensitivity and care she brings to all her inspirational work with people living with dementia. Through Nicky, I have met some extraordinary people who showed me what it means to live well with dementia. Their stories and suggestions and those of their supporters run through the play. Thank you to Mick and Lyn Haith, Eugene Harris and Diana Smith-Harris, Wendy Mitchell, Rosa Peterson, Debbie Catley, Ray and Eileen Chadwick, Bob Fulcher, Pete Grogan, Jan Ellis, Peter and Nancy Jervis and Debbie Marshall.

For their input and support, thank you to Matt Applewhite, Andy Borman, James Brining, Natalie Davies, Alex Ferris, Cathy & Sean Forde, Nikolai Foster, Jacqui Honess-Martin, Tyrone Huggins, Arthur Hughes, Amy Leach, Morven McElroy, Eileen O'Brien, Elizabeth Poet, Peter Poet, Richard 'Ipanema' Poet, Daniel Poyser, Douglas Rintoul, Gilly Roche, Maggie De Ruyck, Janet Stirk, Roger Stirk (still very much treasured), Susan Twist, Sarah Liisa Wilkinson and Christopher Wright. For their talent and all round brilliance, thank you to Shireen Farkhoy, Maxine Finch, Mark Holgate, John McArdle, Anna Marshall and especially, Jemima Levick – I'd trust you with my life. And to Eithne Browne, who read Maggie so perfectly from the roughest draft onwards that I can't imagine her being played by anybody else – thanks for bringing our Maggie to life.

*F.P.*

*For my best friends since forever,*
*Ellie and Beccy.*

**Characters**

MAGGIE, *sixty-seven*
GORDON, *sixty-six*
MICHAEL, *thirty-five*
CLAIRE, *late twenties*
JO, *sixties/seventies*

**Note on Play**

*Maggie May* is designed to be watched by the broadest possible
audience, raising awareness for an audience that aren't directly
affected by dementia, and offering a mirror for people living with
dementia and their supporters alike. Attempts have been made to
ensure the piece is fully dementia-friendly, including the
integration of singing and elements of repetition to enable all
audiences to follow and enjoy the narrative. Maggie's
assessments in **bold** are projected to act as a visual prompt
through the scene. Scene headings may also be projected if useful.

*This text went to press before the end of rehearsals and so may
differ slightly from the play as performed.*

## WAKE UP MAGGIE

*Out of space and time.*

MAGGIE. Eyes send message to brain. Chink of light through the curtains.

**Morning.**

Who am I today?

Sudden snort from the lump lying next to me. Me husband. He doesn't snore. He snorts. These sudden panicked in-breaths through the nose that wake me from the deepest of sleeps. Not that I sleep much these days.

I found him slumped in the bathroom. 'What's happened to you?' He looks up at me, all confused and says summat that sounds like, 'Where's your domino?' 'I don't know, love, but if it's childhood games you're on about, I reckon we should start by looking for your marbles.' Where's your domino?!

'Your husband's had a blockage.'

'Don't talk to me about his blockage. I've been telling him for forty year, he should start his day with a bowl of All Bran.'

'Not a blockage of the bowel, Mrs Morris. The brain.'

'I know all about that an' all. He's had a blockage about using washing machine our whole marriage.'

'Your husband's had a stroke.'

'I know, love. What drugs are you giving him to make him well again because humour's all the medicine I got?'

That bloke of mine doesn't half pick his moments. Must have thought I were getting all the attention.

**OUR GORDON**

*She goes to* GORDON *and gently strokes him awake.*

GORDON. Wake up, Maggie May.

MAGGIE. I'm awake, you big dafty. It's you needs to wake up.

    MAGGIE *helps* GORDON *to sitting and starts putting his slippers on him.*

    And it's Maggie Taylor, ta very much.

GORDON. Maggie Morris last time I checked.

    MAGGIE *stops dressing* GORDON.

MAGGIE. Morris. Of course…

    *A beat.*

GORDON. I gave you a 'silly' surname, I know. Not 'elegant' like some posh gentlemen's tailor. I gave you some berk prancing about at solstice jangling bells.

MAGGIE. Maggie Morris…

    GORDON *sings the first line of Rod Stewart's 'Maggie May'. This spurs* MAGGIE *into action again and she finishes putting his slippers on and gets him into his dressing gown.*

    Pack it in, you.

    GORDON *continues to sing.* MAGGIE *picks up on the reference to being back at school…*

    Oh aye? School is it?

    *As* GORDON *sings,* MAGGIE *laughs at the idea that he is 'being used'.*

    Ha!

    GORDON *continues with* MAGGIE *joining in on the final line of the chorus.*

    Bloody stupid song.

GORDON. It's perfect for you.

MAGGIE. How do you work that out?

GORDON. You're me older woman.

> GORDON *starts the second verse with its reference to* MAGGIE*'s age.*

MAGGIE. Charming! Sixteen months between us. I'm hardly a flippin' cradle snatcher!

Come on, let's get you downstairs. I'll make us some pancakes and you can have breakfast in your PJs.

GORDON. You see ideas like that is why I married you.

> MAGGIE *helps* GORDON *out of bed. A note floats down from the sky in front of her. She picks it up and reads.*

You and your notes. Can't move a step without tripping up on one.

MAGGIE. Why didn't you tell me?

GORDON. Tell you what?

MAGGIE. That it's today our Michael and Claire are coming.

GORDON. Claire?

MAGGIE. His new girlfriend.

GORDON. Is that today?

MAGGIE. Fat lot of use you are.

Hurry up then, I've to get mi'sen organised. I'll start by getting you dressed.

GORDON. Thought it were pancakes in me PJs?

MAGGIE. Not flippin' now it's not!

## OUR BEST FRIEND, JO

JO. Well, are you going to invite me in then? Or have I called at a bad time?

JO *is waiting for a response from* MAGGIE. MAGGIE *is pulled into the present moment.*

MAGGIE (*internal*). Eyes send message to brain. Woman. Brain waits for recognition.

**Jo. Best friend since forever. The most aggravating woman in the world.**

You allus call at a bad time, Jo Stark. Come in then if you're coming.

JO. There's a welcome.

MAGGIE. What is it you want?

JO. To see you.

MAGGIE. Go on then. Take a good look.

JO. To talk to you.

MAGGIE. Talk then. But do it quick because I've a lunch to cook.

JO. Didn't invite me.

MAGGIE. And yet you're here anyway…

JO. Didn't reckon you'd be up to cooking for anybody with your Gordon…

MAGGIE. He's fine.

JO. I've been worrying about you.

MAGGIE. Have you?

JO. I have tried to help, Maggie. But you hardly ever return me calls or texts.

MAGGIE. Takes me too long to write a flippin' text message. Can't be bothered with them. Quicker to phone.

JO. But you don't phone! And when I phone you and suggest us doing summat together, you've a list of excuses long as your arm.

MAGGIE. Have you come round to give me a rollocking?

JO. No! But it's been months so I've come round to see if I can help. If not by doing summat then by distracting you, giving you a laugh.

MAGGIE. Go on then. Give us a laugh.

JO. Put me on the spot, why don't you. Um. Alright then. Did you know that there is a tradition after a bullfight in Spain, to serve the mayor the bull's testicles? One day after a bullfight, the mayor asks the waiter: 'Funny, why are they so small · today?' 'Today, sir, the bull won.'

MAGGIE. That the best you can do?

JO. Well, how about this – Sheila's got a fancy man.

MAGGIE. Her Harry only died last year…

JO. He's the plumber that installed her new bathroom and the best bit is, this new bloke's called Harry an' all.

MAGGIE. No!

JO. She's going round calling him H2. Lots of eyebrows raised.

MAGGIE. If he were my plumber fancy man, I'd call him H2O…

JO. That's good that is. I'll tell her that! Oh, I've missed you, Maggie.

MAGGIE. Missed you an' all.

JO. Has it been very hard? With Gordon.

MAGGIE. Scary at first but not too bad. Allus needed looking after – nowt new there. Physio says he could be back to his old self if he'd just stick at his exercises.

JO. Leave him to fend for himself, that'll give him some incentive. Now what about this quiz? I've left you loads of messages about it. Geoff's quiz master again this year and he's allus a right laugh. Are you in? We can't win it without you.

MAGGIE. I can't.

JO. But you're our secret weapon.

MAGGIE. Weren't last time, were I?

JO. You were… not yoursen that night.

MAGGIE. Who was I then?

JO. Look I don't know what happened. You avoided me for ages after that night.

And then Gordon had his stroke and things have been… well, I've just not seen you. And I hate that. Come on, Maggie, say yes. Sheila'll be there with H2O.

MAGGIE. H2O?

JO. Her Harry.

MAGGIE. Sheila's Harry? He's dead, Jo. You and me went to his funeral.

JO. Her plumber! What the heck, Maggie. Did you get up on the wrong side of the bed this morning?

MAGGIE. Probably. You know me, I'm not a morning person. And I'm worrying about this lunch.

JO. Who's coming?

MAGGIE. Our Michael. It's his birthday.

JO. He's not still cross with you for mucking up his accounts?

MAGGIE. Course not. Should be though. I told him I were on it and I weren't.

JO. How long did he think Mummy should be doing his accounts for?

MAGGIE. Be nice. I were happy to do it. I love a spreadsheet me.

JO. Why'd you pack it in then if you love it so much?

MAGGIE. I don't know, Jo.

JO. Becoming an habit, giving things up. Our shopping trips, book club. Given up loads of things. That's why I never see you.

MAGGIE. Gordon needs me –

JO. Gave it all up before Gordon's stroke. That's probably what caused it – you hanging around the house too much.

MAGGIE. Charming. Stop mithering me.

JO. I'll stop mithering if you say you'll come to the quiz with us. All you need to do is get yoursen to my house at six o'clock on Friday. I'll drive us.

MAGGIE. Write it down for me then. The details.

JO. You'll come?

MAGGIE. I'll think about it. Paper and sticky there. Put a question mark at the end – haven't said I'll come for sure yet.

JO *writes the details on a sticky.*

JO. Done. Where do I put this then?

MAGGIE. Give it here.

MAGGIE *sticks it somewhere. Notes fall from the sky.*

JO. What's with all the notes?

MAGGIE. Nothing.

JO. They're everywhere. What are they all for?

MAGGIE. They're just little reminders. That's all.

JO. You can use your phone for that, you know. You can write your whole shopping list.

MAGGIE. Do you know that's not a bad idea. I do have summat you could help us with if you want to.

JO. I keep offering!

MAGGIE. Can you set me reminders on me phone for all these things?

MAGGIE *passes* JO *a notebook with the relevant page open.*

I've written the timings down here see and what needs to go on at what stage.

JO. Why've you got a reminder for every stage of cooking your ham?

MAGGIE. I just want to get it right.

JO. He's not that fussy is he, the birthday boy?

MAGGIE. He's bringing his girlfriend for us to meet for the first time. We've hardly seen him since they got together. He even spent Christmas at hers. I'm guessing he's fallen hard.

JO. Hope he doesn't bugger it up again.

MAGGIE. Be nice.

JO. What's she called?

MAGGIE *thinks*.

You've not forgotten? That won't make a good first impression!

MAGGIE. Claire!

JO. It is a forgettable name to be fair – Claire. That rhymes that does. Claire, to be fair, has got nice hair.

MAGGIE. She might. He hasn't said nowt about her hair.

JO *is still entering the reminders*.

JO. Have either you or Gordon been reading me blog? I sent you the link.

MAGGIE. I don't really get it, Jo, if I'm honest. Who wants to read you rambling down t'interweb?

JO. Last one were read by sixty-three people!

'Ask Michael how he's finding his new Nissan?' You written out a recipe for the conversation an' all?!

MAGGIE. Just in case it's awkward. Put it in will you.

JO. You wanting me to put all these in? Ask Claire where her parents live. Ask Claire what sort of music she likes.

How bad are you expecting the conversation to be?

MAGGIE (*accessing a rage we've not seen before*). Some people don't talk as much as you do, Jo. Some conversations are two way, need some thought, not like chelpin' to you when you don't shut your gob for two seconds!

*A moment.* JO *is hurt.* JO *enters the reminders in silence.*

Sorry. Jo. I'm sorry.

*When* JO *has finished, she passes the phone back to*
MAGGIE.

JO. There you are. Done.

MAGGIE. Thank you.

JO. Don't need to thank me. I'll see you at the quiz.

MAGGIE. Jo, I didn't say I definitely would –

JO. That's how it works, Maggie. Friends do things for each
other, remember. Or should I be setting a reminder for that
an' all?

MAGGIE. No.

JO. See you on Friday, then.

## BATTLE READY

GORDON. Fifteen minutes.

MAGGIE (*internal*). Eyes send message to brain. Hunched-up
shape of a man I love. Recognition.

**Gordon. Husband. Recovering from a stroke.**

GORDON. Fifteen minutes. If birthday boy's on time. Jacket?

MAGGIE. Alright, bossy boots.

*She helps him into his jacket.*

GORDON. Are we pretty much ready?

MAGGIE. Born ready.

GORDON. Battle ready.

MAGGIE. Steady on, Gordon. Who are we waging war against
– ham in orange and polite conversation?

GORDON *finds a note in his jacket pocket.*

GORDON. What's this? Did you put this here?

MAGGIE. What's it say?

GORDON. It says 'Check outfit.' Well, will I do?

MAGGIE. You'll do. What about me?

GORDON. Most beautiful woman in the world.

MAGGIE. Alright, alright. I don't need speeches. Am I dressed okay? Nowt in the wrong order or inside out. Does everything go together okay?

GORDON. You're fine.

MAGGIE. You've not looked.

GORDON. You look perfect.

MAGGIE. Right.

> MAGGIE*'s phone buzzes with a reminder.* MAGGIE *checks it.*

> Leeks. Better get them on.

> MAGGIE *notices the notes.*

> Oh hell, we need to hide all them notes.

GORDON. No we don't.

MAGGIE. Of course we flippin' do. Get them down or our Michael will think summat's up.

GORDON. He must know summat's up.

MAGGIE. He doesn't.

GORDON. Well he should.

MAGGIE. Leave him be. He's a lot on his plate.

GORDON. We've got to tell him eventually.

MAGGIE. Why?

GORDON. Because we won't be able to avoid it, will we?

MAGGIE. Not today. It's his birthday.

> *The doorbell rings.*

> Oh flippin' heck, they're early.

(*Shouted to the door.*) Just a minute!

MAGGIE *frantically collects up stickies and notes spread about the place.* GORDON *starts to sing 'Give Me Just a Little More Time' by Chairmen of the Board.*

No flippin' time for singing.

GORDON *continues.* MAGGIE *picks up the song and they take a line each,* MAGGIE *taking lyrics which force home the point that they are too short on time to make any mistakes or act foolishly. They end the song in unison.*

*Keys in the door,* MICHAEL *lets himself and* CLAIRE *in.* CLAIRE *wears gold trainers.*


## BIRTHDAY BOY SON AND HIS NEW GIRL

MICHAEL. Are you ready for us?

MAGGIE. Course we are! Come in, come in. You must be Claire.

CLAIRE. So lovely to meet you at last.

CLAIRE *holds out her hand to shake* MAGGIE*'s.*

MAGGIE. Get away with you. I'm not shaking your hand like a bank manager – give us an hug.

*She hugs her.*

Now, let's have that coat off you. Michael, don't just stand there.

MICHAEL. Do I not get an hug then?

MAGGIE. Course you do. Come here. Happy birthday, lad.

CLAIRE. Hello, Mr Morris, I'm Claire.

GORDON. Hello, love. Call me Gordon.

CLAIRE. Lovely house.

MAGGIE. Thanks, love.

MICHAEL. Alright, Dad. How are you getting on?

GORDON. Better thanks, son. On the mend now. How's business? You missing me?

MICHAEL. What's to miss? You bossing me about while I do all the work? Clients miss you, right enough.

GORDON. You having a good birthday?

MICHAEL. So far.

MAGGIE. Card and gift in one.

MICHAEL. Cheers, Mam. It's perfect.

CLAIRE. How do you know?

MICHAEL. 'Cause they always buy me the same thing. A Jumbo Records voucher.

MAGGIE. It's all you ever say you want.

CLAIRE. I brought *you* something actually.

MAGGIE. Oooh, gifts all round.

CLAIRE. It might be a bit… But Michael said you don't get gardeners flowers or plants because you'll always get it wrong.

MAGGIE. He's right there. Gordon is very particular about flowers.

GORDON. And some of the plants we've been given over the years. Bought from a supermarket, half dead. It's like giving a vet a poorly pet for a gift.

MICHAEL (*to* CLAIRE). You see!

CLAIRE. Well, chocolates felt a little impersonal so…

*She presents a wrapped gift.*

MAGGIE. You needn't have bothered, love. Really.

MAGGIE *opens it. It is a full set of Harry Potter books. All seven of them.*

Oh.

CLAIRE. It's the complete set.

MAGGIE. That's…

GORDON. Harry Potter – isn't that for kids?

MAGGIE. …lovely. Really kind of you.

CLAIRE. Oh no, I mean kids love them but there's so much more to them than that.

MICHAEL. Claire's Potter mad, aren't you?

CLAIRE. Just a bit.

MICHAEL. She wrote her uni dissertation on it. Didn't you?

CLAIRE. Book Seven!

MAGGIE. Well, there's a thing. Why don't you sit down?

CLAIRE *takes a seat.*

Michael, love, will you pour the drinks. There's a bottle of red open on the table. Do you like red?

CLAIRE. Love it.

MAGGIE. Glass each of that then. Thanks, love.

MICHAEL *gets the drinks.* MAGGIE *notices* CLAIRE*'s trainers.*

Flipping heck, they're some trainers, girl.

CLAIRE. Do you like them?

MAGGIE. Do I like them?! Me eyes are too dazzled to take them in. Need me shades on.

CLAIRE. Oh, sorry.

MICHAEL. She's kidding.

MAGGIE. Am I?

CLAIRE. They are a bit bright.

GORDON *is looking at the Harry Potter book set.*

GORDON. Didn't love the films, I have to say.

MAGGIE. When have we watched the films?

GORDON. They allus show one at Christmas, don't they. Them
little folk with hairy feet travelling to some wizard mountain.
Hibbits.

CLAIRE. Hobbits? That's not actually –

MICHAEL. That's *Lord of the Rings*, Dad.

GORDON. Is it?

MICHAEL. Harry Potter's the one with the glasses and the scar.

GORDON. Has it got that bloke in it with the holes for a nose.

MICHAEL (*carrying over the drinks*). Voldemort?

GORDON. That's the one. And them black shadowy things
what suck out your soul.

CLAIRE. Dementors.

MAGGIE. What are they?

*An atmosphere change as* CLAIRE *describes the Dementors.*
MAGGIE *feels like this is a description for her alone. She
hangs on* CLAIRE*'s every word, terrified.*

CLAIRE. They're these dark, cloaked skeletal creatures who
float about the world. And when they come close to you,
everything goes cold. As ice. They suck all the joy away, all
the memories, all the bits that make you, you. They eat up
the very essence of you. Every last bit. Suck it all away.
Until you're nothing but an empty body.

*Snap. The warmth comes back into the room.*

But they're not in it until Book Three anyway.

*Normality once more. But* MAGGIE *is slower to recover.*

GORDON. Well, I didn't like them much.

CLAIRE. The films are good and everything but they're not
a patch on the books. They miss out so much good stuff.

MICHAEL. You alright, Mam?

MAGGIE. Course. Why wouldn't I be?

(*To* CLAIRE.) Thank you, love. We'll enjoy working through them right enough.

MICHAEL. You have to read them though. Not just say you will.

CLAIRE. It's a two-part gift you see.

MICHAEL. Claire managed to get tickets for *The Cursed Child*.

GORDON. What's that when it's at home?

CLAIRE. It's the West End show. It carries the story on from Book Seven.

MICHAEL. She's been trying to get hold of tickets the whole time I've known her.

CLAIRE. Every three months they release more tickets and this time I was nine hundred and twenty-seventh in the queue.

GORDON. Must have been standing there ages if you had time to count every bugger in the queue in front.

MICHAEL. It's online, Dad.

CLAIRE. And I knew I stood a chance because the other times I'd been on, my queue number was into the thousands.

MICHAEL. She sat with her laptop on her knee for ninety minutes. Then I hear this huge whoop and she got them.

CLAIRE. Five of them. For me and Michael. My dad and you, if you want to come.

MAGGIE. Not your mam?

MICHAEL. Claire's mam's not…

CLAIRE. Cancer.

MAGGIE. Oh dear. I'm sorry, love.

GORDON. Terrible thing cancer.

CLAIRE. It was nearly five years ago now so, you know…
I'm okay.

MAGGIE. Oh, but you never stop missing your mam.

CLAIRE. No.

I still feel a bit gutted when I phone home and it's my dad that answers. I love my dad and everything… but he's not much of a talker. Anyway, are you up for it then? The show?

MAGGIE. When's tickets for? Better check if we're free.

CLAIRE. April 2021.

MAGGIE. Two thousand and twenty-chuffing-one. You like to plan, don't you?

CLAIRE. They're all sold out before then.

GORDON. Booking summat for your boyfriend and his folks a year in advance. Bit confident that.

CLAIRE. How come? Oh, yeah, see what you mean. 'Cause he might chuck me before then.

GORDON. Or you might chuck him.

MICHAEL. Alright, nobody's chucking anybody, ta very much.

CLAIRE. Didn't really think about it. I suppose I just figured we would still be together next year.

MICHAEL. Me too. Definitely.

GORDON. You hearing this, Maggie? She's here to stay, this one.

## COOKING LIKE ME LIFE DEPENDED ON IT

*Out of space and time.*

MAGGIE. Ham in orange were the first meal I made for
Gordon's parents. Playing houses in us new home and it
seemed such an exotic meal to serve. A bit showy. Well,
cooking a recipe for the first time's torture, isn't it?

Like dancing with your shoes on the wrong feet. I overcooked
the broccoli, cream in the leeks curdled and them roast spuds
wouldn't have crisped up if I'd dropped them in hell fire... but
the ham were perfect. Caramelised and sweet and salty and
delicious and Gordon's mam were ever so impressed.

It became my dish then. Me signature. Our Michael didn't
have any choice but to like it. He allus asks for it on his
birthday. And that suits me fine because when I cook it, it's
like I'm dancing. I know the recipe that well. I don't even
need to engage me brain. I just let me body do what it needs
to. Like it's all choreographed already.

But today it's like I'm starting from scratch. I'm a girl again
in mine and Gordon's first home and I don't want his mam to
think he's picked a duff one so I'm cooking like me life
depended on it. Me shoes both on the wrong flippin' feet.

## GETTING IT WRONG

MICHAEL. Mam?

MAGGIE (*internal*). Eyes send message to brain. Me lad and
a lass with gold trainers at my gaff. Recognition.

**Our Michael's birthday. New girlfriend. All of us trying
to impress each other. Awkward as hell.**

Yes, love.

MICHAEL. Claire was telling you about her job.

MAGGIE. Were you, love?

CLAIRE. No worries. I was boring myself.

MICHAEL. Don't say that. You weren't being boring. Mam's being –

MAGGIE*'s phone buzzes. She reads it.*

MAGGIE (*to* CLAIRE). Don't stop.

CLAIRE. It's really not that interesting. I was just saying, there's three managers in our department and I'm responsible for keeping the diaries of –

MAGGIE. How's the new Nissan, Michael?

MICHAEL. Mam, Claire's talking!

MAGGIE. Of course. Sorry, love. What were you saying?

CLAIRE. Well, I keep the diaries for –

MAGGIE*'s phone buzzes. She reads.*

MAGGIE. Carrots! Excuse me.

MAGGIE *exits.*

MICHAEL. Go on…

CLAIRE. Well, I keep the –

GORDON. She keeps the sodding diaries, Michael. Give her chance to breathe, will you.

MICHAEL. Alright!

CLAIRE. It's quite a fun office to work in. We bring in baking every Friday on a theme. This week was comic books and this one lad went to town and did this amazing Wonder Woman pavlova.

GORDON (*distracted*). That's nice, love. (*To* MICHAEL.) Go easy on your mam, will you, Michael.

MICHAEL. Why? What's up with –

MAGGIE *enters.*

MAGGIE. Now then, where were we? Emily, you were telling us about your job.

*Uh-oh…*

What?

MICHAEL. Mam!

GORDON. Claire.

MAGGIE. What about her?

GORDON. Not Emily.

MAGGIE. No. No! Of course not.

CLAIRE. Who's Emily?

MICHAEL. Nobody.

MAGGIE. It's primary you teach, isn't it?

MICHAEL. Mam, no. That's Emily, not Claire.

CLAIRE. Who's Emily?

MICHAEL. Me ex.

CLAIRE. Oh.

GORDON. Lovely lass.

MICHAEL. 'Sake!

MAGGIE. Oh dear.

> *Awkward as hell is underlined on the projection. MAGGIE gets out some scribbled notes from her pocket.*

How's the new girlfriend, Michael? Is it running well?

MICHAEL. What?

MAGGIE. Nissan. The new Nissan!

MICHAEL. It's grand, Mam. Claire's dad helped me pick it out. He's a bit of an expert, isn't he?

> *MAGGIE's phone buzzes. She reads it.*

MAGGIE. How's the new Nissan, Michael?

> *Desperate to detract from MAGGIE's meltdown, GORDON starts singing 'Hooked on a Feeling' by Blue Swede. The 'ooga-chaka' opening makes quite an impact. Everybody looks a bit shocked but GORDON continues undeterred.*

CLAIRE. Is he alright?

GORDON *continues with his 'ooga-chaka' chant.*

Is he having some sort of fit?

*The ridiculous intro finally done,* GORDON *launches into the song.*

MICHAEL. They do this. Sorry.

MAGGIE *picks up the second verse, her gratitude to* GORDON*'s rescue evident in the lyrics about everything being all right 'in your arms'.* GORDON *takes on the 'Hooked on a Feeling' chorus and an eager* CLAIRE *picks up the following verse supported by* GORDON, MAGGIE *and, eventually, a reluctant* MICHAEL.

*All four sing to the end of the song in unison. A big finish. What now? Bit awkward.* MAGGIE*'s phone buzzes.*

MAGGIE. That's the carrots done.

## OUR MICHAEL

*Out of space and time.*

MAGGIE. His skin were that soft when he were born. I'd lift him up when I were changing his nappy and nuzzle me face in his belly.

I had him on a Thursday. Thursday's child has far to go. You're telling me. That boy. He's a long way from realising his potential, that's for sure.

Barely see him from one month to the next. Even when his dad's had a bloody stroke. If I'd held on till Friday I'd have got 'loving and giving'. Just think.

If he gets the right lass by his side, he will go far, my lad. I know it. And at least I didn't have him on a Wednesday. I'd take 'far to go' over 'full of woe' any day. All I want is for him to be happy.

You're their whole world when they're tots, aren't you?
Once you've had that – them looking up at you like you're
their everything – you'd do owt to protect them and keep
them happy. Even lie.

## DINNER'S RUINED

*All are seated and tucking in.*

CLAIRE. This is delicious, Maggie.

MAGGIE (*internal*). Eyes send message to brain. Who the hell
is that sitting at me table?

**Our Michael's new girlfriend. Birthday lunch. Don't
mess it up.**

CLAIRE. Michael told me you were a great cook.

MAGGIE. Away with you. He just likes what he's used to,
that's all.

MICHAEL. She were a dinner lady for forty year.

MAGGIE. Well, even the best dinner lady can't make school
dinners taste like an home-cooked meal.

MICHAEL. I hoped it'd be ham.

MAGGIE. It's his favourite. Allus have it on his birthday.

CLAIRE. He told me. Must get the recipe.

MICHAEL. You won't find it. It's all in Mam's head. No leeks?

MAGGIE. Leeks?

MICHAEL. Creamy leeks. You always do them with the ham.

MAGGIE. Leeks!

   MAGGIE *looks crestfallen.*

MICHAEL. That's the best bit.

GORDON. Meal doesn't need them.

CLAIRE. It's delicious.

MICHAEL. How could you forget the leeks?

MAGGIE. I, I…

GORDON. She didn't forget. I told her not to bother. Now, give over about bloody leeks will you?

CLAIRE. I'm always forgetting things. I've told Michael – I need a Pensieve!

GORDON. A what sieve?

CLAIRE. Pensieve. Dumbledore's got one. You use your wand to pull out your thoughts and memories and you put them in the Pensieve so you can order your mind and revisit your memories. Wouldn't that be great in real life?

GORDON. She didn't forget.

MAGGIE. Who's Dumbledore?

MICHAEL. Harry Potter.

GORDON. You weren't lying about her being, what did you call it? Potter-mad. Mad as a mad potter's tea party this one!

MAGGIE. Where do your parents live, Claire?

CLAIRE. My dad lives in Otley.

MAGGIE. And your mam?

*An awkward silence.*

CLAIRE. My mum's…

MICHAEL. Mam! Claire's already told you. Her mam's –

GORDON. Oh, Maggie.

MAGGIE. Sorry. I. What did I say?

GORDON. It isn't working. It's worse this way.

MAGGIE. Don't, Gordon.

MICHAEL. What's going on?

MAGGIE. Please. We're nearly done. I'll shut up and make the coffees.

MICHAEL. Why are you both being so weird?

GORDON. We've been living with some difficult news, Michael, for a little while now and your mother doesn't want you worrying but it's time now that you know.

MICHAEL. What is it?

GORDON. Maggie...

MAGGIE. Don't...

GORDON. Alzheimer's.

MICHAEL. Is that what caused the stroke?

GORDON. Not me. Nowt wrong with my brain what weren't allus wrong with it.

MAGGIE. Me.

MICHAEL. What?

MAGGIE. I went to the doctor after I messed up with your accounts. I just couldn't do it. The numbers were swarming everywhere. I couldn't hold it in me head.

And they said then I had what they call cognitive impairment but that it could be caused by depression so I took the pills they gave me and spent a year trying to think mi'sen happy. But when they did more tests, turned out happy had nowt to do with it and it were then they said... Alzheimer's.

(*To* CLAIRE.) So I'm sorry if I've been rude today, love. I've been trying so hard to keep it all together but turns out I'm as demented as them spooky things in your books.

CLAIRE. Dementors.

MAGGIE. That's the one. Them soul suckers. They're after me. In fact, there's a good chance I'll have lost it completely before it's time to go to see *The Cursed Isle* or whatever it's called so as sweet a gesture as it was, I wouldn't waste the ticket on me. (*To* MICHAEL.) I'm sorry, love.

MICHAEL *looks from his father to his mother, totally betrayed.*

MICHAEL. Fuck this.

MICHAEL *storms out. Leaving* CLAIRE *sitting with* MAGGIE *and* GORDON. *An awkward moment.*

GORDON. Did you want a coffee, love?


## THURSDAY'S FLIPPIN' CHILD

*Out of space and time.*

MAGGIE. He's never been good with illness, our Michael. When me mother were dying, he cried if I made him come to the hospital with me. Didn't want to give her a kiss or owt. They were so close but he couldn't bear to see her like that. He were the same with me when I were grieving her. Couldn't deal with seeing me upset so he just… stayed away. And he wonders why I didn't tell him sooner. He's Thursday's flippin' child alright…

MAGGIE *changes into her outdoor shoes.*


## WAR IS NOT THE ANSWER

MAGGIE *and* GORDON *have arrived at* MICHAEL'*s house.* CLAIRE *watches on awkwardly.*

MICHAEL. It's not a good time.

MAGGIE (*internal*). Eyes send message to brain. This isn't Jo's?

**Our Michael's house. First time I've seen him since he found out.**

Thought you were dropping me at Jo's? Gordon?

GORDON. This is more important.

MAGGIE. She'll be expecting me.

GORDON. She won't. You never said you'd definitely go. And you and our Michael need to talk.

MAGGIE. He doesn't want to. Said it's not a good time. He's got his Emily with him.

MICHAEL. Claire!

CLAIRE. Don't not talk on my account.

MICHAEL. Can't talk 'cause I've two hedges to cut while it's still light. And anyway, Mam's the one doesn't want to talk. When I phoned, Dad told me you wouldn't speak to me.

MAGGIE. That sounds… it weren't like that.

MICHAEL. How were it then, Mam?

MAGGIE. I hate flippin' phones. Everything's too quick when you're on the phone.

MICHAEL. How's it quicker than a normal conversation?

MAGGIE. I don't know. It just is. No time to think of what you want to say. Just say owt because person on the other end is waiting for you to say summat. I can't talk to you about *this* on the phone. Your dad asked you to come round and see us so we can look each other in the eye and talk properly.

MICHAEL. It's always on your terms. Everything's a big secret until you're ready to talk about it. Then I have to drop everything.

MAGGIE. It weren't about secrets. It were about not wanting to worry you.

MICHAEL. Well, now's not the time. I've work to do.

GORDON. If you'd half a brain in your head, you'd have known anyway.

MICHAEL. How? How was I supposed to know?

GORDON. Doesn't take a genius. You can even see it in her eyes.

MAGGIE. You what?

MICHAEL. I knew she were a bit off but I thought it were 'cause of you. Your stroke.

GORDON. You thought she were struggling to cope 'cause of my stroke?

MICHAEL. I suppose.

GORDON. So why didn't you offer to help more?

MICHAEL. 'Cause I were working flat-out, weren't I? One-man band with you laid up.

MAGGIE *drifts towards* CLAIRE.

MAGGIE (*to* CLAIRE). I seem to be surplus to requirement in this conversation.

CLAIRE (*to* MAGGIE). Me too.

GORDON. Clients would have understood if you'd explained.

MAGGIE (*to* CLAIRE). Could get a suntan off of them trainers.

MICHAEL. But I needed the money didn't I?

MAGGIE (*to* CLAIRE). That the sole coming off them?

CLAIRE (*to* MAGGIE). Yeah.

MICHAEL. I'm still paying back what it cost me when Mam messed up me accounts.

GORDON. And why do you think she couldn't do the accounts?

MICHAEL. I didn't know, did I?

CLAIRE (*to* MAGGIE). I've only had them four months. Never had them off my feet to be fair. Your Michael bought them for me.

MICHAEL. I can't do this now.

GORDON. Whose hedge are you cutting? I'll call them. Give us your mobile.

GORDON *holds out his hand for* MICHAEL*'s mobile*. MICHAEL *hesitates*.

CLAIRE (*to* MAGGIE). I feel all shiny when I wear them. Pretty much how I feel when I'm with him. Most of the time.

MICHAEL. Not your client to call no more.

MAGGIE. That's how I used to feel with our Gordon.

Neither of them making me feel very shiny just now. (*Projects this so the men hear.*) Talking about me like I weren't even here.

*She's got their attention.*

MICHAEL. Just defending mi'sen.

(*To* GORDON.) Telling me I'm stupid for not knowing. What do you want me to say? I'm a shit son. Sorry.

MAGGIE. You are not a shit son!

*That has silenced everybody.*

MICHAEL. You're wearing odd shoes.

MAGGIE. Am I?

GORDON. Thought you went back and changed them?

MAGGIE. I did. Must have changed into another odd pair.

MICHAEL. Bloody hell, Mam.

GORDON. Oi! I remember time were you couldn't fasten your laces. Your mam were right patient with you then. Show her the same consideration, will you?

MICHAEL. What, like she's a kid? She's me mam. And she can't even dress herself properly.

CLAIRE. Don't make a big deal about the shoes, Michael. We're all family aren't we?

MICHAEL. No, Claire. We're not.

CLAIRE *is wounded.*

CLAIRE. No. I'll leave you to it. Sorry.

CLAIRE *exits.*

GORDON. She were right. Lay off your mam. You have no idea what she's coping with.

MICHAEL. No, I don't. Because I've only just found out, haven't I?!

GORDON. No actually. Been best part of a week and you've still not spoken. That's why we're here.

MAGGIE. Leave him, Gordon. Don't have to talk if he doesn't want to.

MICHAEL. It's you that doesn't want to.

MAGGIE. I'm here aren't I?

MICHAEL. Only 'cause Dad tricked you into coming.

MAGGIE. Don't see why you couldn't come to us.

GORDON. Both as stubborn as each other.

MICHAEL. Talk then.

MAGGIE. What do you want to know?

MICHAEL. Dunno. What do you want me to know?

MAGGIE. Dunno.

MICHAEL. How long?

MAGGIE. Nobody really knows, love.

GORDON. Eight to twelve years.

MAGGIE. Flippin' heck, Gordon! Depends on loads of things. How fit you are. How much you keep doing for yersen. It's not fixed. I could still outlive half the people on our street.

MICHAEL. But will it be you?

MAGGIE. Who else would it be?

*The question hangs there for a minute. Neither says anything.*

GORDON. You not got any other questions, Michael?

MICHAEL *shakes his head.*

Must be stuff you want him to know, Maggie?

MAGGIE *shakes her head.*

If you're not going to talk, least you can do is give each other an hug.

MAGGIE. Don't feel much like hugging.

MICHAEL. Me neither.

*Silence.*

GORDON *starts to sing 'What's Going On' by Marvin Gaye, putting real feeling into the lyrics begging 'mother' not to escalate the situation into a war and choose love not hate.*

Not now, Dad.

GORDON *keeps on singing.*

MAGGIE. Gordon…

GORDON *gives it some on the chorus with its repetition of the same question, 'what's going on?' He's building towards something when…*

MAGGIE *and* MICHAEL. Shut it!

GORDON *stops at their outburst.*

GORDON. Least I made you agree on summat.


## QUIZ NIGHT

JO. What are you doing here, Maggie?

MAGGIE *changes into matching shoes…*

MAGGIE (*internal*). Eyes send message to brain. Hurry up, brain – don't leave me hanging.

**Jo. Best friend. Quiz night. Pretending everything's normal.**

Six o'clock. Friday. Your place. You wrote it down. Here I am. You seem surprised.

JO. I am a bit.

MAGGIE. How come?

JO. I… I –

MAGGIE. Have I got summat wrong with me? Is me dress inside out or summat? It can't be me flippin' shoes…

JO. No, you look lovely it's just –

MAGGIE. What? Why are you looking at me all weird?

JO. I thought you'd forget.

MAGGIE. Why would I do that?

JO. Michael phoned me night of his birthday.

*This hangs for a moment.*

MAGGIE (*internal*). Ears send signal to brain. Brain sends it to heart.

**Me son. Told me friend I had dementia. Secret's out.**

He had no bloody right.

JO. He were upset. He feels lied to.

MAGGIE. So he rang you? You do nowt but attack him most of the time. What's he ringing you for?

JO. See if he were last to know. Turns out that were me.

*A beat.*

MAGGIE. His birthday? You've known for five days and didn't think to call me? To visit?

JO. And say what? You clearly didn't want me to know.

MAGGIE. Saying it makes it real. And I didn't want you looking at me different. Like you are now.

JO. How am I looking at you?

MAGGIE. Like I'm a piece of glass you could smash.

JO. I'm sorry. (*Getting upset.*) I'm so so sorry.

MAGGIE. Don't. I've not died. I'm still here.

JO (*through tears*). I know.

MAGGIE. Don't set me off. I don't need to test whether this mascara is waterproof or not.

JO. Sorry.

MAGGIE. Right. Are we going then?

JO. You mean…? I invited Sarah W to join the team. I didn't think…

MAGGIE. Champion. Sarah W may be boring as hell but she's got right good general knowledge.

JO. We're only allowed four in a team.

MAGGIE. Sarah W can boot it then. She's not all that.

JO. You hated it last time.

MAGGIE. Because it were noisy and crowded and I couldn't get me brain to focus.

JO. It'll be the same tonight.

MAGGIE. And yet you wanted me to come.

JO. I didn't know. I thought you had an off night. I didn't realise it was who you are now.

MAGGIE. You what?

JO *realises what she said.*

I said I'd go and I'm going.

JO. Fine. Good. They won't make a fuss about there being five of us. Not if I explain what's going on with you.

MAGGIE. Don't you bloody dare. You want to ask them if it's okay if old half-a-brain here sits on the side quietly. She won't get any of answers any road. I know what, shove me in a costume and I'll be your flippin' mascot!

JO. This isn't you talking.

MAGGIE. Then who the hell is it?

JO. I read up on it. Aggressive behaviour is a symptom of the disease.

(*Whispered.*) Alzheimer's.

MAGGIE. If I could choose what memories I could hold on to, I'd forget every laugh we've ever had and remember how much I hate you in this moment. And it's me saying this, Jo. Not the disease. Me, Maggie. Hating you.

JO. Bloody hell, Maggie, you're as cold as ice.

MAGGIE. You're right. I take it back. I don't want to remember this. You don't deserve the space in me brain.

*She turns to leave, head held high.*

## MAGGIE LOSES HER WORDS

*Out of space and time.*

MAGGIE *approaches the audience as if she's about to talk to them but…*

MAGGIE. –

*…the words don't come. This is confusing and distressing for her.*

## THE FOG

GORDON. You're not ready?

MAGGIE (*internal*). Signals sent. Brain confused.

**Husband. Me. Fog.**

GORDON. You're not ready, Maggie.

MAGGIE. For what?

GORDON. The meeting at the café.

MAGGIE. Who with?

GORDON. You know. Other people like you.

MAGGIE. Everything's foggy today. I can't go.

GORDON. That's why we made such a detailed plan about the day. You've got all the timings written down, maps and pictures. You'll be fine.

MAGGIE. Why do I have to?

GORDON. So you can meet other people going through what you are. Make friends.

MAGGIE. Got enough friends already.

GORDON. Oh aye? Where are they?

*A beat. He's right.*

Get a'gate or you'll be late for your meeting.

MAGGIE. Too foggy today.

GORDON. You've been foggy every day for weeks. You've not been looking after yersen since our Michael's birthday. Not been yersen at all.

MAGGIE. Who've I been?

GORDON. I don't know…

MAGGIE. Who am I, Gordon?

Funny Maggie? Holder of useless facts Maggie? Mam? Dependable Mam, Mam'll do it Mam, holds all the pieces together Mam? Am I still her?

GORDON. Could be if you'd get out of bed.

MAGGIE. Not today. Alzheimer's Mam. Dementia Maggie.

GORDON. You'll go downhill quicker than a greyhound with a jar of mustard if you don't get yersen dressed and face the world. Need to keep doing what you were doing when you were pretending but now you don't need to pretend no more.

MAGGIE. Something's wrong, Gordon. I feel all wrong.

GORDON. You've been right lax about taking your medication…

MAGGIE. Isn't about popping pills. It's getting me. Quicker than they said.

GORDON. Nonsense. Come on, love. Nowt's going to feel right till you start living again…

GORDON *sings 'Stayin' Alive' by the Bee Gees. With his 'Ah, ha, ha's', he sets* MAGGIE *up for the chorus but* MAGGIE *leaves him hanging.*

You know it. Sing it for me.

(*Sings.*) *Ah, ha, ha, ha…*

*Nothing from* MAGGIE.

I don't like leaving you like this.

MAGGIE. Leaving me?

GORDON. I've to get to me physio. Will you go to this meeting or not?

MAGGIE. I can't!

GORDON. Will you be alright on your own? Will you? Maggie?

## CLAIRE VISITS

CLAIRE. Maggie, are you alright?

MAGGIE (*internal*). Message failure.

**Girl. Who is she? Gold trainers.**

CLAIRE. It's me, Claire.

MAGGIE. I'm Maggie… May.

CLAIRE. Maggie Mae. Like The Beatles song?

(*Sings.*) *'Oh Maggie Maggie Mae, they have taken her away and she'll never walk down Lime street any more.'*

Actually think she was a… you know, a woman of the night.

MAGGIE *sits down, slumps a little.* CLAIRE *is still standing looking awkward.*

Are you alright, Maggie? Where's Gordon?

MAGGIE. Gordon had a stroke.

CLAIRE. Another one?

MAGGIE. What?

CLAIRE. Gordon had another stroke?

MAGGIE. Did he?

CLAIRE. I don't know, Maggie. Let me text Michael. You don't seem yourself.

CLAIRE *texts* MICHAEL.

MAGGIE *sings the first line of 'Maggie May' by Rod Stewart.*

I don't know that one.

MAGGIE*'s clutching at her privates.*

Do you need the toilet, Maggie?

MAGGIE. It burns. Burns like a bonfire. I don't know you.

CLAIRE. You do, Maggie. I'm Michael's girlfriend, well –

MAGGIE. Emily?

CLAIRE. No. I'm Claire.

MAGGIE. Where's Michael?

CLAIRE. I don't know, Maggie. Maybe he didn't tell you…? We split up.

MAGGIE. I've a head full of syrup. Need a shower to wash it out. Where's the shower gone?

MAGGIE *starts to wander off.*

CLAIRE. Maybe leave the shower till Michael comes, hey?

MAGGIE. Where's Michael?

CLAIRE. On his way, Maggie.

MAGGIE. Monday's child is fair of face, Tuesday's child is full of grace, Wednesday's child is… is… Wednesday's child is… I don't remember.

CLAIRE. Why don't you sit down, Maggie?

MAGGIE. Why are you here?

CLAIRE. I just came to say… it doesn't matter?

MAGGIE. You selling something? I don't want nothing.

CLAIRE. No. I wanted to let you know that you can keep your tickets. For *The Cursed Child*. If it won't be weird sitting together with me and my dad. You'll like my dad. He's funny like you. Least he used to be.

MAGGIE. Cursed?

CLAIRE. We can talk about it another time. It's not till next year.

MAGGIE. Who's cursed?

CLAIRE. Nobody. Forget it. I mean… sorry.

MAGGIE. Wednesday's child is… what is it?

CLAIRE. I don't know.

MAGGIE. I think you should go.

CLAIRE. I think I should stay. Just until Michael gets here. Okay?

## WHY ARE YOU STARING AT ME?

*Out of space and time.*

MAGGIE. Monday's child is fair of face, Tuesday's child is full of grace. Wednesday's child is… full of woe, Thursday's child has far to go, Friday's child is loving and giving, Saturday's child works hard for his living, and the child that is born on the Sabbath day is bonny and blithe, and good and…

MAGGIE *looks at the audience. Their presence suddenly feels confusing.*

Who are you? Why you watching me? Get your neb out of me business. Stop looking at me. Stop it. Go on. Get out of here.

**BACK WITH CLAIRE**

CLAIRE. I can't go, Maggie. Not with you in this state.

MAGGIE. **Eyes. Brain. Gold. Girl. Who. Help. Burning. Fog. Scared.**

CLAIRE. Let me stay. Just so you're not on your own. I could sing to you, like Gordon does.

CLAIRE *sings 'If You Let Me Stay' by Terence Trent D'Arby.*

Do you know this one?

CLAIRE *continues to sing.* MAGGIE *calms a little.*

That's right. Everything's fine isn't it?

*A* DEMENTOR *appears. It walks towards* MAGGIE. *She cries out, terrified. It's going to suck out her soul. She tries to get away but bumps into* CLAIRE.

What's wrong, Maggie? Where are you going?

MAGGIE *is backing away but it's getting closer and closer.* CLAIRE *hasn't seen the* DEMENTOR *approaching.*

MAGGIE. No. No.

CLAIRE. There's nothing to be scared of.

MAGGIE. Leave me alone. No. NO!

*A* DEMENTOR *no more,* MICHAEL *stands in its place.*

MICHAEL. Mam, it's me. What's wrong? Mam? You're scaring me.

## GIVE US A LAUGH, JO

JO. Hello, Maggie.

MAGGIE (*internal*). Brain signal. Face. Smile. Recognition.

**Hospital. Visitor. Best friend.**

What are you doing here?

JO. Gordon phoned me. You've had an infection?

MAGGIE. Waterworks. Nice of Gordon to tell the neighbourhood about the intricate workings of me bladder.

JO. I'm not 'the neighbourhood'. I'm your best pal.

MAGGIE. –

JO. I were going to ask you how you are but you look a damn sight better than Gordon. You gave him a fright.

MAGGIE. He got off lightly compared with our Michael. He were the last flippin' person I wanted to see me in that state. Couldn't have planned a better way to confirm his worst fears about me diagnosis.

JO. But it weren't the dementia were it?

MAGGIE. Yes and no. Alzheimer's means me brain is juggling two balls in one hand but wang in another ball and they all come crashing down. The infection in me urinary whatsit were a ball too many. Brought on a delirium they call it. Dose of antibiotics and a couple of nights' rest and, bingo, I'm mi'sen again.

JO. Thank God for doctors.

MAGGIE. Oh aye, allus dreamt of snagging yersen a doctor, haven't you, Jo Stark?

JO. Haven't given up hope yet. Why do you think I'm here?

*They share a laugh.*

MAGGIE. We fell out, you and me.

JO. You remember that do you?

MAGGIE. I can feel the knot of it in me belly.

JO. Memory like a bloody elephant, you have. Only plus side I can see of this disease of yours is that you might not remember every bloody cross word.

MAGGIE. I don't remember the words. Just the feeling of it. I remember that it hurt.

JO. Hurt me an' all.

MAGGIE. Sorry about that.

JO. I'm sorry too.

MAGGIE. Give us a laugh, Jo.

JO. Have you heard the one about the woman, call her Maggie, who prayed to God: Dear Lord, please make me win the lottery. The next day Maggie begs the Lord again: Please make it so I win the lottery, Lord! The next day, Maggie again prays: Please, please, dear Lord, make me win the lottery!

Suddenly she hears a voice from above: Maggie, would you kindly bob into the shop and buy yoursen a lottery ticket.

MAGGIE. You can do better than that.

JO. Not sure I can. How are you?

MAGGIE. Better. Though I washed me purse in the sink earlier instead of me hands.

JO. Oh dear. I do stupid things like that all the time. Found me remote control in the fridge!

MAGGIE. Do you forget the kettle has a button to boil water? Do things in cupboards stop existing for you when the doors are closed? Do you forget whole conversations?

JO. I forgot our Janey's birthday. I forgot the name Prince Philip the other day. Just gone. Had to call him the Queen's bloke. It's the curse of age, isn't it?

MAGGIE. No, Jo. That's not what's wrong with me. I'm not forgetful. It's not old age. I have brain disease. Would you visit a friend with stomach cancer and say, 'Oh yeah, I get tummy aches an' all.' No you bloody wouldn't. Unless you get a diagnosis of dementia, please don't compare your scattiness to my life.

JO. Point taken. What's it like then, this disease of yours?

MAGGIE. You really want to know?

JO. I asked, didn't I?

MAGGIE. I just finished first chapter of a book and I'm half expecting Oxford university to award me an honorary degree for me achievement. It were that hard. It were only eighteen pages long, Jo, and written for kids. I used to read an eight-hundred-page historical novel by the second day of me hols. That's what this disease does. It makes ordinary things feel impossible.

Imagine you'd had a right full-on day, your brain's fair thraiped and you're good for nowt but sleeping and somebody starts quizzing you on summat you've not studied since school. That's how much brain energy it takes me to buy summat from the shops. Simplest things need thought and planning. I even have to set mi'sen flipping reminders to eat and drink and when I do, it tastes like somebody turned the volume down on the flavour.

They say we're like swans. Ruddy beautiful graceful things on the surface of a lake but underneath we're paddling like mad. I tell you, if I'd brought the same level of graft to me life before this condition, I could be Prime flippin' Minister. Now, best I can hope for is normal. And do you know what? That feels like I'm aiming too high now. I have to accept I'm never going to finish even one of them Potter books.

Even when me brain's working well, I'm waiting for when it'll let me down again. And every bad day reminds me of where I'm headed and the thought of it –

MAGGIE *stops suddenly. We don't see them but, for* MAGGIE, *the Dementors are present.*

JO. Go on…

MAGGIE. –

JO. Don't stop, Maggie. Tell me.

MAGGIE *banishes the thought of them.*

MAGGIE. I'm done with it. Paddling like some flippin' swan.

JO. A ruddy beautiful and graceful swan.

MAGGIE. More like an ugly duckling.

JO. You can't stop paddling.

MAGGIE. Why not?

JO. Because if you stop paddling, you'll drown. And you and me won't let that happen.

*JO picks up the Harry Potter book from* MAGGIE*'s bed and flicks to the contents page.*

A chapter's a good start. Only sixteen more to go.

*She passes the book to* MAGGIE *who hesitates and then takes it, with a smile – challenge accepted.*

**REMEMBERING THE WORDS**

*Out of space and time.*

GORDON *sings the first verse of 'Let's Stick Together' by Bryan Ferry to* MAGGIE. MAGGIE *picks up the second verse and they continue to pass the song back and forth, finishing in perfect, joyful unison.*

*Interval.*

## WHAT THE FUTURE HOLDS

MAGGIE *enters and makes her way to the hospital bed.*
GORDON *and* MICHAEL *are set apart, both looking
shell-shocked.*

MICHAEL. Bloody hell.

GORDON. I know, son.

MICHAEL. It that what the future holds? Is that how she'll
    end up?

GORDON. Honestly?

    I don't know. Should ask her. Come on.

    GORDON *heads over to* MAGGIE. MICHAEL *follows.*

    Hello, love. You done snoozing? Will have done you good
    that will.

MAGGIE (*internal*). Eyes send message to brain. Bright room,
    smells like antiseptic.

    **Hospital. After the delirium. Mi'sen again. Son and
    husband looking right worried.**

    Alright, Michael.

MICHAEL. Mam.

MAGGIE. Long time since I woke up to your face.

MICHAEL. Yeah.

MAGGIE. Who do I write the letter of condolence to?

MICHAEL. You what?

MAGGIE. Look on your face, I take it somebody died. Just
    wondering who so I can pass on me condolences.

MICHAEL. Nobody died.

MAGGIE. That's a flippin' relief.

    How's that girl of yours? The one with the gold trainers.

MICHAEL. Her name's Claire. And she's not mine any more.
    We split up.

MAGGIE. Why didn't you tell me?

MICHAEL. –

MAGGIE. What did you do?

MICHAEL. If I knew that I could make it right, couldn't I?

*An awkward pause.*

GORDON. Do you want a drink, Maggie?

MAGGIE. Voddy and coke.

MICHAEL. We're in the hospital, Mam.

MAGGIE. I know that. Just trying to raise a flippin' smile.

GORDON. It were frightening, love. Seeing you like that.

MICHAEL. Understatement.

MAGGIE. All sorted now. Nowt to worry about.

MICHAEL *scoffs*.

What?

MICHAEL. All sorted? Bloody trailer of what's to come more like.

MAGGIE. What's that supposed to mean?

MICHAEL. You looked right at me and you didn't recognise me.

*Once again,* MAGGIE *feels the presence of the Dementors.*

MAGGIE. It were the infection.

MICHAEL. You didn't know me, Mam. Not even a flicker of recognition.

MAGGIE. Do we have to talk about this?

MICHAEL. If not now, when?

MAGGIE. I dunno, a week next Tuesday or, let me think... never.

MICHAEL. Mam!

MAGGIE. You think I'll forget you?

MICHAEL. I do now, yeah.

MAGGIE. I will NEVER forget you.

GORDON. Maggie…

MAGGIE. You think I could ever not know me own son? That will never happen.

GORDON. You can't say that, love. You know –

MAGGIE. I do know, Gordon. I know what I know.

GORDON. You won't choose it, love, but the disease…

You won't get a say in what you do or don't remember. Can't promise something like that.

MAGGIE. This is between me and our Michael.

GORDON. Is it? Who'll be picking up the pieces after?

*An impasse. A lot of pain in the room.*

MAGGIE. I had size five feet before I had you. Loads a mams say their feet grow during pregnancy, hormones and water retention, weight gain, but they all go back to their normal size after. Mine never. Size six ever since. Had to bin an whole wardrobe of me favourite shoes because, after having you, none of them flipping fit.

MICHAEL. Another thing I need to feel guilty about.

MAGGIE. Having you changed me. Not just me feet. And I can't change back again. I am your mam as much as I'm me.

And you may be an infuriating little brat at times but I grew you. Not just in me body. Out of it an' all. I've fed you and worried over you and loved you. For the nineteen years you lived at home with us, I looked at your sleeping face last thing before I went to sleep every night. And when you left home, I had to put a picture of you by me bed because I can't sleep without seeing your mug. I dream your face, Michael. I won't ever forget it. I will never not recognise you. You hear me?

MICHAEL *hears her.*

**END-OF-LIFE PLANNING**

GORDON. Where do you want to die?

MAGGIE (*internal*). Eyes send message to brain. Recognition.

**Home. Husband. End-of-flipping-life planning.**

I'm trying to read me book.

GORDON. Got to look ahead while you still can.

MAGGIE (*wilfully referring to her book*). You mean skip to the last chapter – that'd be cheating.

GORDON. Got to face up to what's coming, Maggie. Telling our Michael you'd never forget him?! You can't say things like that.

MAGGIE. Stop mithering me.

GORDON. I want to know what you want.

MAGGIE. I want to get to the end of this book.

GORDON. At the end, Maggie. I want to know what you want at the end.

MAGGIE. I promised our Jo I'd finish it if it killed me. Turns out it might. Keep forgetting who everybody is.

GORDON. Talk to me.

MAGGIE. No.

GORDON. Maggie…

MAGGIE. I said, no.

GORDON. 'Cause you're frightened but you won't admit it.

## CRYSTAL BALL

*Out of space and time…*

MAGGIE. Gordon told me I'd marry him on our second date. I asked him what made him so sure and he told me he had a crystal ball. I said 'Gordon, if you had a crystal ball, you'd sit down very carefully.'

He's allus wanted to look ahead. And I've allus wanted to take life a day at a –

GORDON *stands between* MAGGIE *and the audience.*

GORDON. Don't do that?

MAGGIE. Do what?

GORDON. Disappear on me. Muttering to yoursen. Come back to me. Talk to me.

MAGGIE. I were just thinking how you allus looked ahead. From second time we met.

GORDON. That were never you.

MAGGIE. I'd have liked to have a career as a psychic but…

MAGGIE *and* GORDON. I couldn't see no future in it.

GORDON. I can help you get to the end of your book, if you like.

MAGGIE. I can't see you spending your day reading about witches and wizards.

GORDON. If that's what you want, I'll read you the whole damn set.

MAGGIE. With me asking who everybody is all the time? Stopping and starting. I'll drive you mad.

GORDON. You've been driving me mad from the first minute I saw you, woman, why stop now? I know you don't think you've got choices, Maggie, but I can help make sure you do. If you want to read or go for a walk, you can lean on me.

MAGGIE *scoffs.*

I'm getting stronger. Me physio says if I keep at it, I'll be back the way I were.

And when it gets to the end, I'll make sure you get what you want then too.

MAGGIE. How do you know it'll be me that goes first?

GORDON. I don't.

*A beat.*

MAGGIE. Okay. I'll do it.

But only if you do it too. Deal?

GORDON. Deal.

GORDON *gets his end-of-life planning papers.*

Where do you want to die?

MAGGIE. What are me options? 'Cause if it lists a bejewelled palace with silk sheets, you can tick that. Or a well-heated castle overlooking the sea. Or a warm beach at sunrise. Any of them would do.

GORDON. Home, hospital or hospice.

MAGGIE. Hospice. What about you?

GORDON. Home.

MAGGIE. That's because I keep us home nice and clean. No offence, love, but when I'm about to die, if I've had months of being out of it, this place'll look like a pigsty. An hospice'll be clean and the staff will know better than you how to keep me comfortable.

GORDON. See that's good. I wouldn't have known that.

MAGGIE. Write it down then. Your answer and mine.

GORDON. What about treatments and different types of care?

MAGGIE. I don't want owt will keep me alive artificially if that's what they mean. You wouldn't neither would you?

GORDON. I bloody would. If me heart stops and there's a doctor who can CPR me one more look at your beautiful face, he'd better damn well do it.

MAGGIE. Should have known. Only one thing you'd want people to say at your funeral, Gordon Morris…

GORDON. 'He's moving!'

True that. Can't imagine anything worse than dying, me.

MAGGIE. I can.

*The* DEMENTORS *are back. A physical presence once more.* MAGGIE *backs away.*

It does scare me, Gordon. It flipping terrifies me.

GORDON. I know.

*The* DEMENTORS *circle during* MAGGIE'*s speech. She watches them wearily.*

MAGGIE. I don't want to be a body to be washed and fed. I don't want you having to do that. If I've… gone. But frightens me to think of nurses doing it. 'Cause they won't know who I were. Won't know that I had a sense of humour or that it's me way to be brusque but I love very strongly. I don't want to be a shell. I don't want to stop being me.

GORDON. You'll still be in there.

MAGGIE. How do you know?

GORDON. A woman me mam told me about years ago. Went into a home, mild as anything, became most violent resident they'd ever had. Punching and kicking. Turned out, she were abused as a kid. And when the staff took her into her room to change the dressings of these ulcers on her legs and rolled down her stockings, it brought it all back.

MAGGIE. Why are you telling me a sad thing like that?

GORDON. There's an happy ending. They turned a storeroom into sort of doctor's surgery and made it clear everything were clinical and above board and she didn't fret after that. No more hitting or punching. She were still in there.

The person she were, her memories. You'll still be in there an' all.

MAGGIE. How will anybody know to look that deep to find me?

GORDON. I'll make sure they do.

MAGGIE. How?

GORDON. I'll tell 'em you're a Rosa Eden. All cut back for winter, spiky and thorny with no flowers but I'll explain the flowers were there and they will be again. I'll tell them they just need to be patient and the most beautiful flowers they've ever seen will grow. Same roots, different season.

*The* DEMENTORS *stop circling.*

MAGGIE. Yeah. You tell 'em that.

## EXPECTO PATRONUM – CHASING THE FEAR AWAY

MAGGIE *faces up to the* DEMENTORS *while* GORDON *prepares to read to her. They're close to the end of the third Harry Potter book* – Harry Potter and the Prisoner of Azkaban.

GORDON. Where were we? We read Dementor's Kiss, didn't we? Oh yes, things are hotting up now. The wizard boy's terrified of them spooky things that nearly sucked out his soul last chapter. But he's got a chance now. He tries that Expecto Patronum spell one last time. And it only bloody works. He sends out a silver animal from his wand, which charges at them Dementors.

MAGGIE *walks towards the* DEMENTORS, *who begin to back away.*

And they don't like it. This sleek and beautiful silver creature is stronger than them. They can't suck out its soul because it's not frightened. So they melt away to nothing.

MAGGIE *waves them away with a flourish and they disappear.*

'Bout time them spooky things got their comeuppance, hey? You up to speed now? Shall I start reading?

**GOLD TRAINERS**

MICHAEL. You ready?

MAGGIE (*internal*). Eyes send signal to brain. Ready for what?

**Getting ready to go to the group. Nervous feeling in me belly.**

*During the following,* MAGGIE *gets herself ready, puts some lippy on and changes her shoes.*

Are we late?

MICHAEL. Not yet.

MAGGIE. Don't flippin' rush me then.

MICHAEL. Remind me where I'm dropping you.

GORDON. You're not dropping her anywhere. You're going in with her.

MICHAEL. To meet a load of people with dementia?

GORDON. And their partners.

MICHAEL. Well, I'm neither of them things am I?

GORDON. You're there to support your mam.

MICHAEL. Why aren't you going?

GORDON. I've me last physio appointment halfway through the meeting. Don't make a fuss. It'll be good for you both.

MICHAEL. Sitting in a circle and talking? My idea of hell.

MAGGIE. Mine too.

GORDON. Exactly. That's why you both need to go. You pair are a bloody pain, you know that.

MAGGIE. What've I done?

GORDON. You know damn well. Turning a little trip to the bank into a shopping spree. Reckon you wanted to be late so you could bunk off this thing.

MAGGIE. Would I be that devious?!

GORDON. Do you want me to answer that?

MAGGIE *raises an eyebrow.* GORDON *breaks into 'Devil Woman' by Cliff Richard.*

MICHAEL. Oh, bloody hell.

MAGGIE *picks up the tune but changes the 'she' to an 'I', owning that she is indeed a 'devil woman'.*

You pair are so weird.

MAGGIE. How long have I got?

GORDON. Plenty time but better that way than have to rush. You can have a cake in the café beforehand. Here, lad.

GORDON *gives* MICHAEL *some cash.*

MICHAEL. What's this for?

GORDON. For tea and cake.

MICHAEL. Don't be daft. I can stretch to a slice of cake for me mam, can't I?

GORDON. Take it. Parking in town costs a bloody fortune.

MICHAEL. Put your money away, old man.

How are you getting on, Mam? Let's get off and I'll buy you a millionaire's shortbread.

MAGGIE *emerges wearing bright gold trainers. They look ridiculous.*

MAGGIE. I'd rather have a bag of chips.

MICHAEL. What are them?

MAGGIE. What?

MICHAEL. On your feet?

MAGGIE. Me new trainers.

GORDON. She saw them in the window of that little shop next to the bank and she were in there and had them bought before I knew what were happening.

MICHAEL. This a joke?

MAGGIE. What do you mean?

MICHAEL. They're just like the ones I bought for her.

MAGGIE. Who?

MICHAEL. My ex, Mam, who do you think?

MAGGIE. Emily?

MICHAEL. Claire! Not bloody Emily.

MAGGIE. Oh. Suppose they are. How funny.

MICHAEL. Funny?! Dun't feel very funny to me.

MAGGIE. Thought they were a bold choice but I saw them and had to have them. Must be missing her, I suppose.

MICHAEL. You're missing her?! Called her Emily every time you saw her and you're missing her now.

GORDON. Calm down, Michael.

MICHAEL. *You're* missing her. How do you think I feel?

MAGGIE. I haven't the foggiest, Michael. You ain't said nowt about her. Just another lass you've messed it up with.

MICHAEL. We were fine until you dropped your bombshell!

MAGGIE. Oh, it were my fault were it?! You're not seriously blaming me?

MICHAEL. Not blaming anybody. Saying how it were. One minute everything were good, the next she's on at me for not talking to her. Saying how it's brought back all the memories of her mam and how I'm just like her dad.

MAGGIE. Should have flippin' talked to her then.

MICHAEL. Say that like it's easy.

MAGGIE. It is. Move your lips and let the sound come out.

You're a grown man, Michael. If the lass needs you to talk, you talk.

MICHAEL. I know that now, don't I?

Feel like you're laughing at me, wearing them.

MAGGIE. Course I ain't. I didn't know you were cut up about Claire. Never get more than a grunt from you about it.

MICHAEL. Because I'm gutted about it, Mam. I can't stop thinking about her. Everywhere I go, she's there in me mind. Her smile, her laugh. It's like being bloody haunted. Not by a ghost but by the empty feeling she's left behind.

MAGGIE *wanders to find a notepad.*

Where you going?

MAGGIE. 'Haunted by the empty feeling she's left behind.' Were that it? It were beautiful. Say it again.

MAGGIE *starts jotting it down.*

MICHAEL. Don't laugh at me.

MAGGIE. I'm not laughing.

MICHAEL. What are you doing?

MAGGIE. Writing it down.

MICHAEL. Don't.

MAGGIE *writes.*

I said, don't.

MAGGIE *writes.* MICHAEL *bats the notepad out of her hand.*

Fuck this.

*He storms out.*

GORDON. Michael. Michael!

MAGGIE. I just didn't want to forget what you said.

*But he's gone.*

GORDON. Told you not to buy them trainers.

MAGGIE. You didn't flipping say why.

GORDON. I don't remember what people wear on their feet!

MAGGIE. Will you give me a lift?

GORDON. Course. Glad you're not using it as an excuse to miss it.

MAGGIE. Not to the meeting. Somewhere else.

GORDON. Maggie…

MAGGIE. It's important. You'll see.

## PLAYING CUPID AT CLAIRE'S HOUSE

CLAIRE. Is everything alright?

MAGGIE (*internal*). Eyes send signal to brain. Sweet girl looking confused.

**Me son's ex. Me sticking me neb in.**

Where's your gold trainers?

CLAIRE. I binned them. The soles were coming off and –

MAGGIE. And they reminded you of our Michael?

CLAIRE. Suppose. Also they stank. How are you?

MAGGIE. Better than I were when you last saw me. Thanks for the flowers you sent when I got home from hospital.

CLAIRE. Wasn't sure you'd remember.

MAGGIE. Gordon reminded me on the way here.

*An awkward silence.*

Hardly recognise you now without them trainers.

CLAIRE. Why are you here, Maggie?

MAGGIE. Good question. Probably sticking me neb in where it's not wanted…

CLAIRE. Is Michael alright?

MAGGIE. Not really, love. What about you?

CLAIRE. Not great.

MAGGIE. Our Michael says I'm the reason you two split up.

CLAIRE. Did he say that? Idiot.

*But he's her son…*

Sorry.

MAGGIE. Don't apologise to me. I agree. He's a right idiot.

CLAIRE. He's right in a way. He just shut down when he found out. My dad did the same when my mum got her cancer diagnosis. He still can't talk to me about her. I love your son, Maggie, but I'm not strong enough to have two men in my life who shut me out.

MAGGIE. I don't blame you, love. Gordon would say that's my fault an' all. Me and Michael like us emotions the way posh people like their water – bottled.

CLAIRE *laughs*.

CLAIRE. I didn't want to end it. Thought it might force him to open up. Fight for me. But he just let me go. Suppose he didn't feel as strongly about me as I did him.

MAGGIE. I don't mean to be rude but you're dead wrong there, love. I've summat you need to read.

MAGGIE *retrieves her notepad and tears out a page, which she passes to* CLAIRE.

CLAIRE. What is it?

MAGGIE. Our Michael said it about you.

CLAIRE. Did he?

MAGGIE. When he broke up with Emily, we were gutted. She were that lovely. I mithered him something ridiculous about that girl, how he should win her back, but he kept saying he weren't that bothered that it had ended. I've never heard him speak like that – (*Points at the note*.) about anybody, love.

You keep that and have a think about it. I might have a gift for you an' all. What size feet have you? Tell me you're a six.

CLAIRE. I am. Yeah.

*Delighted,* MAGGIE *hands over a box*.

You shouldn't have bought me anything.

MAGGIE. I didn't. I bought them for me. And I look flippin' ridiculous in them.

CLAIRE *opens the box and brings out the gold trainers.*

CLAIRE. These are just like my ones.

MAGGIE. Didn't realise what made me buy them at first. I've become a right impulsive shopper since me diagnosis – should see the fluorescent kilt I bought last month. But I reckon there's a reason I bought these. It's because I wanted something shiny in me life. Not shoes though. The lass that wears them who has the shiniest smile I've ever seen. That's what I want in me life. In me son's life.

CLAIRE *starts to cry.*

What've I said? Are you crying?

CLAIRE. That's just the nicest thing anybody's ever said to me.

MAGGIE. Don't be daft. Stop that, you silly thing. You're going to make me late – can't leave with you bawling your eyes out.

CLAIRE. Where are you going?

MAGGIE. This group of other folk with me condition. Our Gordon's set on me going. You can take somebody with you but Gordon's busy and our Michael – well, that's a different story.

CLAIRE. Want me to come?

MAGGIE. You wouldn't want to come along to summat like that.

CLAIRE. Why not? If you want the company…

MAGGIE. I flippin' do.

CLAIRE. Well then…

MAGGIE. It'll probably be awkward as hell. Standing round, nobody knowing what to say to each other.

CLAIRE. Sounds just like when I visit my dad. It'll be a story to tell anyway, won't it?

MAGGIE. So long as we survive it.

CLAIRE. I'd better put my trainers on so you remember who I am. Don't want you introducing me as Emily.

MAGGIE *likes this flash of attitude*.

MAGGIE. As if I would.

CLAIRE *puts on her trainers*.

You know what you should do with your dad. Cook him summat your mam used to cook. That'll get him talking. Powerful thing, food. For them that remember to eat and can taste the full flavour.

CLAIRE. Dad always did the cooking. Mum was a terrible cook.

MAGGIE. She must have made something. What were her signature dish?

CLAIRE. She did make kebabs for the barbecue. Dad would always cook them but putting them together was her thing.

MAGGIE. Can you make them like she did?

CLAIRE. Think so. You really think it'll get him talking about her?

MAGGIE. As sure as eggs is eggs.


## AFTER THE FIRST GROUP MEETING

GORDON. Told you so.

MAGGIE (*internal*). Brain. Message. Recognition.

**Me and me son's ex sharing us stories about the support group. Husband smiling. Smug git.**

Alright Mr Knowitall. You didn't tell me they'd get me writing a poem!

CLAIRE. Maggie's face, when they suggested it, was a picture.

MAGGIE. I've never written a poem in me life and I'm not going to start now!

CLAIRE. Except you did!

MAGGIE. I wrote song lyrics. Different.

CLAIRE. It was lovely. All about you.

GORDON. Me?

CLAIRE. About how you've finished each other's songs all your marriage. And how even when she's feeling foggy and can't find any words, she can always manage to finish the song you start for her.

MAGGIE. Shhh. Don't be giving him a big head. This one woman got really into it. Wrote this thing with a fair bit of salty language in it.

CLAIRE. The woman with the hair?

MAGGIE. Pink stripe down it.

CLAIRE. Hers was hilarious.

MAGGIE. She were a right laugh. Oh and get this. She showed me dress she were wearing – it's reversible! So there's no getting it inside out. It's fog-proof. Going to get me a wardrobe full so I don't need to check all my outfits with you any more.

GORDON. Still need me to check if you've got it stuck in your knickers, mind.

MAGGIE. You probably wouldn't even notice. Do you know, Claire, he let me go out one day with only half a face on. Me eye make-up were done ever so beautifully but only on one flipping side!

CLAIRE. Gordon!

GORDON. I don't notice stuff like that.

MAGGIE. Anyway, this Sandra had loads of great tips. What about that app she were talking about?

CLAIRE. It's for the kitchen. It's short films of how to do simple things like brew a tea or make cheese on toast.

MAGGIE. Makes sure you get everything in the right order. Sandra said it were right helpful. Anyway, she goes to this other meeting on a Monday so I figure I'll try that an' all.

Stop looking so smug, you.

GORDON. Why would I be smug? Only been telling you for months that you'd love it and now been proved right.

MAGGIE. Shut it.

CLAIRE. Tell him about the blog.

MAGGIE. One of them writes one – says it acts as a memory for her. Typing up what's happened, who she's met, that sort of thing. Thought I might ask our Jo to set me up with one.

GORDON. Who'd want to read that?

CLAIRE. I'll read it.

GORDON. Brace yourself, love. Our Maggie's no J.K. Rowling.

MAGGIE. How do you know?! Might be. Wednesday – Gordon heated up me favourite soup and then we sat down for a nice lunch with Voldemort.

*Their laughter is interrupted by the sound of keys in the door. MICHAEL walks in. He takes in the assembled group, his jaw dropping at the sight of CLAIRE. They all look a little like children caught doing something naughty...*

GORDON. Michael.

MAGGIE. Hello, lad.

CLAIRE. Hi.

MICHAEL. Alright.

I came back to take you to your group but you'd gone.

MAGGIE. Claire went with us.

MICHAEL. Why?

CLAIRE. Why not?

MICHAEL. How'd it go?

MAGGIE. It were grand, yeah.

CLAIRE. Your mum was brilliant.

MICHAEL. I would have taken you. I weren't going to miss it. Just needed to kick off some steam.

MAGGIE. It's alright, love. Worked out better really. Having Claire with me. You'd have stood making me feel twice as awkward. She walked right in and introduced herself to everybody, chatty as anything. Made it easy on me.

MICHAEL. She's good at talking, is Claire.

CLAIRE. Only when people talk back.

*Awkward…*

MICHAEL. I'll take you next week, Mam. If you're going back?

MAGGIE. Would you?

MICHAEL. Can't promise I'll say owt.

MAGGIE. Folk don't allus have to talk. Sometimes just being there is enough.

*A shared something between* MAGGIE *and* MICHAEL.

Only problem is one or two of them got into their heads Claire were me daughter.

MICHAEL (*playful*). Want me to borrow one her frocks so folk think I'm her?

MAGGIE. That would make it simpler for everybody.

MICHAEL. Don't want to confuse the group…

GORDON. Oh aye, you in a frock is much less confusing.

CLAIRE. I'll pick you something out.

MICHAEL. I've got the legs for it anyway.

CLAIRE. True. But not the arse.

MICHAEL. Oy. What's wrong with me arse?

CLAIRE. Nothing. Except when you start talking out of it.

MICHAEL. Rude, that is.

CLAIRE. Just teasing you…

> *A shared something between* MICHAEL *and* CLAIRE *that* MAGGIE *and* GORDON *enjoy watching.*

> What are you doing now?

MICHAEL. Dunno. Why?

CLAIRE. Just wondered if you could give me a lift home?

MICHAEL (*a little over-eager*). Yeah. Yeah I could.

> Unless you want me to stay, Mam. I owe you a bag a chips.

MAGGIE. We can do that any time, lad. You get off.

## WHO DIED?

JO *stands over* MAGGIE *and* GORDON *who are both weeping and occasionally laughing through their tears.*

JO. What the hell is going on? Has summat bad happened?

MAGGIE (*internal*). Brain sends message.

**Me and me husband crying us hearts out…**

GORDON. No.

> MAGGIE *cries some more.*

JO. Maggie?

MAGGIE. No. Everything's fine.

> GORDON *and* MAGGIE *laugh through the tears.*

JO. Thought somebody had died.

MAGGIE. They did.

> *She bursts out crying again.*

JO. Will somebody tell us what's happening?

MAGGIE. Cedric died.

JO. Who did?

GORDON. Cedric.

MAGGIE. Voldemort killed him.

JO. I don't know what you're on about.

GORDON. Harry Potter.

> *Projection changes to **Me and me husband crying us hearts out… about Harry Potter.***

JO. You're beefin' over Harry Potter?

MAGGIE. It was just so unexpected. Poor lad. He were just a kid.

JO. Have you forgotten about the quiz?

GORDON. We haven't forgotten. Just got carried away finishing Book Four. You're all ready to roll aren't you, Maggie May?

MAGGIE. I think so.

> MAGGIE *gets a tissue, wipes away her tears and gives her nose a good blow.*

Are you sure you want me on your team? Didn't you win last year?

JO. Because Sarah know-it-all W knew all the answers. She also sucked the fun out of everything. I'd rather come last and have a laugh with you. Time for a brew before we go. Thought I might check your blog page while I'm at it. How are you getting on with it?

MAGGIE. Okay, I think. It's a good excuse to get things down so I can remember them. Even if nobody reads it.

GORDON. No can do on the brew front I'm afraid.

JO. Why's that?

GORDON. No kettle.

MAGGIE. Some bugger zapped it in the microwave.

JO. Who did?

MAGGIE. Who do you think? I just wanted to make the water warm. I watched it sparking and everything. Buggered up the kettle AND the microwave – no brew for us.

JO. Maggie!

MAGGIE. I know. Wouldn't believe I used to manage a kitchen that made over five hundred meals a day.

JO. Is your computer on or have you paggered that an' all?

MAGGIE. Help yoursen.

*JO exits, leaving* MAGGIE *and* GORDON *alone.*

Did summat bad happen?

GORDON. Eh? No.

MAGGIE. I feel like it did. Big sinking feeling right here. I don't think I can go tonight.

GORDON. Course you can.

MAGGIE. I've got this heaviness. Sadness here. What's caused that? What's happened, Gordon? It doesn't feel right. I won't go. Summat's wrong.

MAGGIE *is getting distressed.*

GORDON. Hey, hey! Maggie. Be reight.

GORDON *sings 'I'll Be There' by The Jackson 5.* MAGGIE *is calmed by it and joins in, taking alternate verses and ending together.*

There, see. You'll enjoy it tonight. Go and get your coat on so you're ready.

MAGGIE. Yeah.

MAGGIE *goes to leave.* GORDON *sits down on the Harry Potter book, realises and laughs and calls after* MAGGIE.

GORDON. Summat bad did happen.

MAGGIE. Why are you laughing then?

GORDON. Cedric. Cedric died.

MAGGIE. Who's Cedric?

> GORDON *is lost for words at this. How can she have forgotten so soon? He starts to cry. It surprises both of them. He's not crying about Cedric, or that she forgot the treasured moment of finishing the book together, but all the little daily losses, all the panics and worry.*

> Gordon? What's wrong? Are you alright? What's wrong?

> (*Calling off.*) Jo, summat's up with Gordon. Come down quickly.

> GORDON *is weeping now but pulls himself together in time for* JO's *entrance.*

JO. What's up?

GORDON. I'm fine. I just… I'm fine. You girls should get off to your quiz. Maggie, I'm fine. Get your coat on.

JO. Gave me a fright.

MAGGIE. Are you sure you're alright, love?

JO. He's fine. Any road, I've a bone to pick with you, Mrs.

> JO *ushers* MAGGIE *to the door and helps her into her coat.*

> Your blog's got three times as many readers as mine. Three times!

MAGGIE. Has it really?

JO. You've only been doing it a couple of months.

GORDON. It's all her new pals.

MAGGIE. A few of them have blogs linked to me so I'll have got people who read theirs reading mine, I suppose.

JO. Typical. Never blogged in her life. Starts and she's a hit. It's galling, that's what it is. Are we ready then?

MAGGIE. Ready. We won't be back late, Gordon, and then maybe you can read me some more of the Harry Potter. We've only got a couple of chapters to go, haven't we?

## SUNSHINY DAY

GORDON. Sounds like a right productive morning.

MAGGIE (*internal*). Eyes send message to brain. Recognition.

**Reporting back to me husband on me new job. Dementia
Ambassador. Proud of mi'sen.**

So they're wanting us on the advisory board to have a gander
round the new facilities to assess how dementia-friendly they
are. But Wendy's raging that they didn't ask us at the design
stage. Because she says that's when we can really make a
difference. As it is we're mostly focusing on signage.

There's never enough. Speaking of which, our ensuite...

GORDON. What about it?

MAGGIE. I keep telling you once the door's shut, that
bathroom stops existing for me. Have to peg it downstairs
for a wee because I've forgotten there's a toilet right next to
us bed. And yet you keep closing the door.

GORDON. You've been telling me for forty-odd years to shut
it. Wish you'd make your mind up.

MAGGIE. Well, you can keep it shut now. I'm going to sort out
some signage of me own. Wendy talking about the bog
cubicles and how flippin' hard it is to find the exit again,
gave me a eureka moment.

Stop smiling at me like a dafty. Just 'cause I'm firing on all
cylinders.

GORDON. Makes me happy. One of your sunshiny days.

MAGGIE. It is. No fog at all. Which is not what I thought
would happen at half four this morning when I were
wandering around not able to sleep. Any road, meant I got
mi'sen organised for today.

GORDON. Today?

MAGGIE. You haven't forgotten? Why don't you roll over to
my side of the bed and see what me notes for the day say?
Our Michael's birthday.

*Heading changes to **Our Michael's birthday.***

GORDON. Course it is.

MAGGIE. They're coming over at…

*She checks her phone.*

In ten minutes in fact.

GORDON. Why so early?

MAGGIE. Our Michael and Claire are doing the veg – I'm teaching them how to cook me leeks.

GORDON. You're not letting them cook your ham?

MAGGIE. Course I'm bloody not. Give them chance to walk before we ask them to run. I'll do the ham. I'm that relieved that today's a sunshiny day.

GORDON *sings 'I Can See Clearly Now' by Johnny Nash.*

Oh here it comes.

*She joins in and finishes with a big bright 'sun-shiny day'.*

Do we have to sing this every time I have a good day?

*But* GORDON*'s not finished yet. He starts on the second verse.*

Oh we're dancing now are we?

*They sing together until the doorbell rings.*

Oh hell. They're here.

GORDON*'s still singing.*

Let go of me. I need to answer the flippin' door.

MAGGIE *makes for the door while* GORDON *sings on, key change and everything.*

*Keys in the door.* MICHAEL *lets himself and* CLAIRE *in before* MAGGIE *can get to the door.*

MICHAEL. You ready for us?

GORDON *doesn't answer but continues the verse.*

Hey up, is he singing again?

MAGGIE. Happy birthday, love.

MICHAEL. Thanks, Mum.

GORDON *is finally hitting the end of the song, building to the last, joyful line which* CLAIRE *jumps in with…*

CLAIRE (*sings*). *Sun-shiny day!*

MAGGIE. Very nice, love. Come on in.

CLAIRE. Hi, Maggie. Brought some chocolates for you.

GORDON. What, no more books you want us to read?

MAGGIE. I hope not. We're stuck on… Which one is it, Gordon?

GORDON. Book Five. All eight hundred pages of it.

CLAIRE. Oh dear. It's worth it though. Keep on going.

GORDON. Have to don't we if we're coming with you to see the big show.

MAGGIE. Now then, birthday boy, I've got summat for you.

MICHAEL. Thanks, Mam. I love me a Jumbo Records voucher.

MAGGIE. Eh? Is that what we normally do?

MICHAEL. Like every year.

MAGGIE. Oh. Well not this year. Hope you like it.

MAGGIE *hands a wrapped box to* MICHAEL, *which he unwraps.*

MICHAEL. A Polaroid camera. Cheers Mam. Thanks Dad.

GORDON. Your mam chose it. Got it into her head.

MAGGIE. Your dad had one when we first met. You look right like him standing there holding that. Just need the flares.

GORDON. And the rugged good looks.

MICHAEL. Oi, what you saying? I'm better looking than you.

CLAIRE. I'd better get started on the veg. What should I be doing about these leeks?

MAGGIE. Chop them in half and quarters and then slice them about that big. Now then, I've written a list. You'll need to cut some garlic, grate half a block of cheese and get some thyme from the garden. Then I'll tell you what's what.

CLAIRE. Right then. On it.

*CLAIRE exits.*

GORDON. I'll get me good shirt on.

*GORDON exits. MICHAEL sits down and opens his new camera, setting it up.*

MAGGIE. You not helping her? Thought I were teaching you two all me recipes before they disappear.

MICHAEL. Claire's on it.

MAGGIE. What if she chucks you? What'll happen to me recipes?

MICHAEL. She's not going to chuck me.

MAGGIE. Make sure of it, lad. Don't want a repeat of what happened with Emily.

MICHAEL. When are you going to stop going on about Emily?

MAGGIE. When me condition spreads to the Emily part of me brain. Then I'll forget she ever existed.

MICHAEL. Hurry up and forget then will you.

MAGGIE. I'm working on it.

*A moment.*

About that. Happens I told you summat that weren't a lie but close to it. Summat I shouldn't have promised. About the future and you and me. Will you ask me, so I can answer it better?

MICHAEL. Don't spoil today.

MAGGIE. I might not remember next time. And some days the words just won't come. Ask me. Please, Michael.

MICHAEL. Will you forget me?

*The questions sits heavy in the air.*

MAGGIE. I hope not. But I might.

MICHAEL. I don't want you to.

MAGGIE. I don't want to.

MICHAEL. I hate it.

MAGGIE. Me too.

> Thing is, Michael, even if the day comes when I don't
> recognise you. If I don't know your name and I can't place
> who you are. That's just me brain. Me heart will know. I'll
> feel the love. I might not know why but I'll feel it. I'll feel
> you. And just being in the same room as you will make me
> happy. In me heart. I don't know much but I know that.

MICHAEL. I love you.

MAGGIE. I know, sweetheart. But it's right nice to hear you
say it.

*The doorbell rings.*

> That'll be our Jo. You get it and I'll show Claire what's what.

MAGGIE *exits.* MICHAEL *opens the door and takes
a Polaroid of* JO.

JO. Oh Michael, you gave me a right fright then.

MICHAEL. Sorry, Auntie Jo.

JO. Alright, love. Happy birthday. Didn't know what to get you
so I got you a voucher for Jumbo Records.

MICHAEL. Perfect, thanks.

JO. Where is she then?

MICHAEL. Teaching Claire all she knows in the kitchen.

JO. Shouldn't take too long then. I'm kiddin'! Did she tell you
she won the quiz for us?

MICHAEL. No.

GORDON *enters.*

GORDON. She told me hundred times. She were that chuffed.

JO. We were neck and neck with another team and she were the only one who knew the answer to the tiebreaker.

MAGGIE *enters*.

Ambersummat, wasn't it?

MAGGIE. Ambergris. Whale vomit. Used in perfume.

MICHAEL. How did you know that?

MAGGIE. I've no idea. It were just there. Only answer I knew the whole night.

JO. Bloody tiebreaker. Our hero.

CLAIRE *has entered*.

MICHAEL. Did you hear that, Claire?

CLAIRE. Amazing!

MAGGIE *greets* JO *properly*.

MAGGIE. Hello, love.

JO. How are you today?

MAGGIE. Sunshiny.

JO. Thought so. You look bright-eyed.

MAGGIE. But shh, don't say it to Gordon or he'll start singing again. And you'd be amazed how many songs he knows with sunshine in the title.

GORDON. 'You Are My Sunshine.'

MICHAEL. 'Sunshine of My Life.'

CLAIRE. 'Bring Me Sunshine.'

JO. Oh, I can't think of one.

MAGGIE. Good, I don't need you to start an' all. Right then, Claire and me have got how many minutes till we've to be back in that kitchen?

CLAIRE. Twenty.

MAGGIE. Give us a laugh, Jo.

JO. She allus puts me on the spot. Well, I've got one for you today. Doctor has to break some bad news to his patient.

He steels himself and comes straight out with it: 'I'm very sorry to have to tell you, you've got cancer and Alzheimer's.' To the doc's surprise, the patient looks relieved and says 'Well, doctor, at least I don't have cancer.'

*A shocked silence from the assembled group. Has* JO *misjudged it terribly and then, just as the tumbleweed might have blown,* MAGGIE *starts to laugh, long and hard. She's tickled pink by that. Her laughter's irresistible so they all start laughing with her. They've forgotten what they're laughing at now but it feels good and then…* MAGGIE*'s not laughing any more, she's crying.*

Are you beefin'?

GORDON. Are you alright, love?

MICHAEL. Mam?

JO. First time I've told a joke so bad it's made you cry.

MAGGIE. It's not that. It's this. Being with you all. It's bloody brilliant. I want to keep hold of it and I know I can't. Our Michael standing there with his camera in his hand looking just like Gordon did when I met him. How long until I forget that? A day, a few hours? How long until I forget what Gordon even looked like back then? How long until I forget all of you?

*A moment. Nobody knows how to answer this. The Heading changes from* **Michael's Birthday** *to* **Pensieve – A Magic Way To Save Memories**.

CLAIRE. We need Dumbledore's Pensieve, don't we?

MICHAEL. Not sure it's the moment for Harry Potter, Claire.

GORDON. She's right. Give me a minute.

GORDON *goes to retrieve something.*

JO. What's he doing?

MICHAEL. Don't ask me?

*GORDON returns with a toolbox. He swipes away clutter from the coffee table and empties the toolbox onto the floor. He slams the toolbox onto the table.*

GORDON. That is a Pensieve.

*He rifles through the tools and presents* MAGGIE *with a screwdriver.*

And this is your wand.

MAGGIE. What am I supposed to do with this?

GORDON. Pull out the memories with that and put them in there. Anything you know you want to keep. Go on.

MAGGIE. With everybody watching?

GORDON. That's the point. We're all here and want to know what memories you need to keep. Go for it.

MAGGIE. Alright. Well, the one I said of you in your flares with your camera in your hand. Actually, it was over your shoulder on a strap. The night we first met at that dance and we'd spoken and I'd told you me name but then we got split up and I were sorry because I liked the look of you and then Rod Stewart came on. 1971. 'Maggie May'. It were a new song. I'm not sure if I'd even heard it before that night. But you came walking up to me and said 'Alright, Maggie May, shall we dance?' And that were that.

GORDON. Put it in then.

MAGGIE. How?

GORDON. Pull it out of your head. That's right. I can see that now. Silvery flame memory – (*Looks to* CLAIRE.) that's right, isn't it?

CLAIRE. Yeah.

GORDON. And put it in the box.

MAGGIE *does.*

Do another one then. That worked that did, didn't it? It's in there now. I could see it.

CLAIRE. Yeah. Just like magic.

MICHAEL. You've all gone daft.

MAGGIE. Our Michael's first laugh. The sound of it. His little
face. I were pulling faces. Hoped to get one of his smiles. I'd
have done anything for one of them smashing smiles. So I'm
pulling faces and suddenly this giggle. I can hear it now.
Most beautiful sound in the world.

GORDON. Put it in then.

MAGGIE *puts it in*.

JO. What about us? Can I get in there an' all?

MAGGIE. Oh yeah. Um. I know! We were having a coffee
before doing the dinners and this young teacher comes in
wanting an early lunch because he's invigilating later on and
you run around sorting him out and set him up on the same
table as us. And you're smiling and listening to him like he's
the most interesting person in the world and then he says
summat that's one of them double entrendres, doesn't mean
to but you catch my eye and you burst out laughing and
coffee spurts through your nose onto his dinner. I've never
seen you blush redder than that.

JO. Don't put that in. Of all the memories, of all the laughs
we've had, that's what you choose to put in. Don't. Maggie.

MAGGIE. I'm putting it in. It's going in.

JO. I said don't. Maggie!

I don't know why I'm bothering. It's a screwdriver not
a bloody wand.

MAGGIE. There's good magic on this screwdriver and you
know it. That memory's in there for the rest of time.

JO. Ooo, Maggie Morris, you're a stinker, you are.

GORDON. What else?

MICHAEL. What about Claire?

MAGGIE. Well, I'd put this in. Today. Her learning me recipes
and all of us having a laugh. But there's no point trying to

keep hold of it. The new stuff just goes. I'll remember the feeling of it. I just wish I could keep the pictures too.

GORDON. Put it in anyway.

CLAIRE. Might work.

JO. Good magic and all that.

MICHAEL. No. It won't work.

JO. Michael!

MICHAEL. But this will.

MICHAEL *holds up his Polaroid camera, they all squeeze together and* MICHAEL *takes the selfie.*

MAGGIE. Let's see it then.

MICHAEL. Give it a minute.

JO. Think me eyes were closed.

MICHAEL *flaps it around to get the image to appear.* MAGGIE*'s phone buzzes.*

MAGGIE. Leeks.

CLAIRE. On it! Michael, can you pick me some thyme from the garden?

GORDON. I'll make us some tea.

GORDON *exits.*

MICHAEL. Which one's thyme again?

JO. Call yoursen a bloody gardener.

MICHAEL. I just get it mixed up with rosemary. Anyway, I do hedges mostly, don't I?

JO. Come on, I'll show you.

MICHAEL *passes* MAGGIE *the photo.*

MICHAEL. There you go.

MAGGIE. That's lovely. Thank you.

MICHAEL. Put it in the box then.

*She does and closes it tight shut.*

JO *and* MICHAEL *exit.* CLAIRE *hovers.*

CLAIRE. I finally made the kebabs for my dad.

MAGGIE. What kebabs, love?

CLAIRE. The ones my mum used to make. You told me to. A while back now but there hasn't been a day sunny enough for a barbecue. First sign of sun last weekend, I did it.

MAGGIE. I told you to make your dad kebabs. Why the hell did I do that?

CLAIRE. You said it would get him to open up so we could talk about my mum.

MAGGIE. Did I? And did it get him talking then?

CLAIRE. No. He burst out crying.

MAGGIE. Oh hell.

CLAIRE. Halfway through eating it, he turned away from me and I could just see his shoulders bobbing up and down. He was sobbing his heart out.

MAGGIE. I'm sorry, love.

CLAIRE. No, it was good. I nestled in to him and he hugged me in the tightest hug and we both just cried for ages. I don't think he'll ever be able to talk about her. But it's like you said to Michael, isn't it? People don't always have to talk. Sometimes just being together is enough.

MAGGIE. I think so. I hope so.

CLAIRE. Anyway, just wanted you to know. I'd better get on with these leeks.

CLAIRE *leaves.* GORDON *comes back with a cup of tea for* MAGGIE.

GORDON. What you smiling about?

MAGGIE. I did a good thing, Gordon.

GORDON. Good for you.

MAGGIE. Do you know, I think I may still be able to… even with this disease.

GORDON. What?

MAGGIE. Change things for the better.

GORDON. You may do anything you set your bloody mind to, Maggie May.

*He gives her a kiss and exits to the kitchen.* MAGGIE *lifts up the closed toolbox Pensieve and opens it. Magic happens. Silver flame memories dance about her. She breathes them in. She picks up the picture and smiles.*

*Blackout.*

**A Nick Hern Book**

*Maggie May* first published as a paperback original in Great Britain in 2020 by Nick Hern Books Limited, The Glasshouse, 49a Goldhawk Road, London W12 8QP, in association with Queen's Theatre Hornchurch, Leeds Playhouse and Curve Theatre, Leicester

*Maggie May* copyright © 2020 Frances Poet

Frances Poet has asserted her right to be identified as the author of this work

Cover artwork by Feast Creative

Designed and typeset by Nick Hern Books, London
Printed in the UK by Mimeo Ltd, Huntingdon, Cambridgeshire PE29 6XX

A CIP catalogue record for this book is available from the British Library

ISBN 978 1 84842 951 2

**www.nickhernbooks.co.uk**

facebook.com/nickhernbooks

twitter.com/nickhernbooks